To Longrain staff: past, present & future

Published by Periplus Editions (HK) Ltd.,
with editorial offices at 130 Joo Seng Road #06-01,
Singapore 368357

First published in 2003 by Hardie Grant Books
85 High Street, Prahran, Victoria 3181, Australia
www.hardiegrant.com.au

www.longrain.com.au

ISBN-13: 978-0-7946-0487-5
ISBN-10: 0-7946-0487-0

Photography by Jeremy Simons
Photography assistance by Mark Garrett
Text design by text-art

Distributed by

North America
Tuttle Publishing
364 Innovation Drive, North Clarendon, VT 05759-9436 U.S.A.
Tel: 1 (802) 773-8930; Fax: 1 (802) 773-6993; Email: info@tuttlepublishing.com; Website: www.tuttlepublishing.com

Japan
Tuttle Publishing
Yaekari Building, 3rd Floor, 5-4-12 Osaki, Shinagawa-ku, Tokyo 141-0032
Tel: (81) 3 5437-0171; Fax: (81) 3 5437-0755; Email: tuttle-sales@gol.com

Asia Pacific
Berkeley Books Pte. Ltd., 130 Joo Seng Road #06-01, Singapore 368357
Tel: (65) 6280-1330; Fax: (65) 6280-6290; Email: inquiries@periplus.com.sg; Website: www.periplus.com

Printed in Singapore

10 09 08 07
 6 5 4 3 2 1

Modern **Thai** food

100 Simple and Delicious Recipes from
Sydney's famous Longrain Restaurant

by Martin Boetz

15 contemporary cocktails and wine tips
by Sam Christie

Foreword by David Thompson

Photography by Jeremy Simons

PERIPLUS

Contents

I am delighted to write this introduction to the international edition of Martin Boetz's book, *Modern Thai Food*.

A visit to Longrain Restaurant and Bar in either Sydney or Melbourne, Australia, will quickly show any visitor the deft cooking skills of Martin Boetz, which are mixed with fantastic service and glamorous cocktails! It is this combination of quality and attention to detail mixed with big servings of fun that makes Longrain's restaurants so incredibly successful.

However, what makes Longrain truly popular is Martin's cooking. It is a singular blend of Thai and modern Australian food. Martin has evolved this intricate style over many years and his talent was immediately apparent when he started as an earnest young cook in my kitchen at Darley Street Thai. Since opening his own restaurant with Sam Christie several years ago, Martin's talent has been acknowledged internationally to general acclaim.

Now with the release of this mouth-watering cookbook everyone has the chance to cook and taste why Longrain and Martin's food are so admired. Get cooking and sample some of Martin's luscious *Modern Thai Food* for yourself!

David Thompson

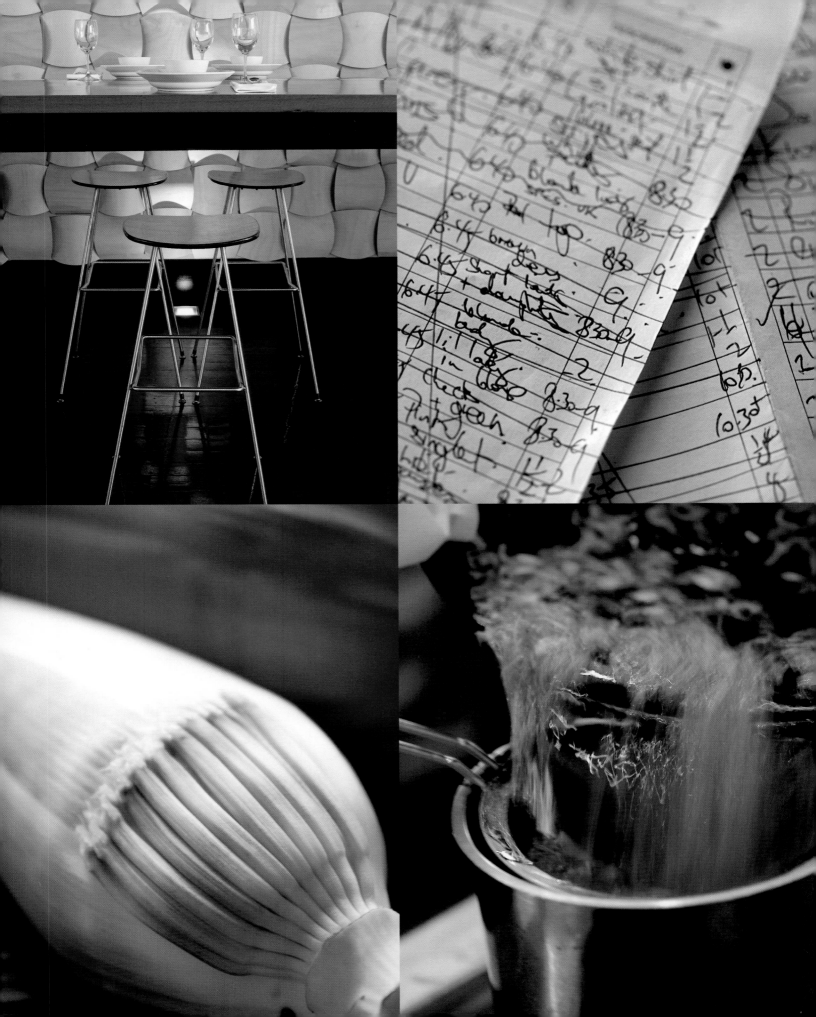

Welcome to Longrain

Longrain (pronounced long grain) is the name of our restaurant in Surry Hills, Sydney, which opened on 27 August 1999. While some of the recipes here are typical of the food that you will find in the restaurant, this is a book written for the home kitchen and the home cook.

German boy, Asian food . . . it's not an association that springs readily to mind, and a testament to Australia's diversity that chili and fish sauce happen to do it for me more than olive oil and balsamic vinegar. Thai food is the food I most enjoy eating and creating; I love the flavors, and working to bring out the best combinations. For me, the smells of Thai basil, kaffir lime leaves and chili just call to be mixed into a stir-fry of duck and chili jam—I can imagine the finished dish even as I put the basil into the bag at the market. Other people play golf or paint; balancing flavors is my creative pursuit. I've been cooking Asian food for over ten years now, and I hope to keep doing it for a while more—there's still so much left to learn about the flavor combinations, ingredients and cooking techniques.

My love affair with Thai food began at Darley Street Thai in Sydney's Kings Cross. I was totally blown away by the restaurant and the range of amazing flavors in the food. The first time I went there with Katrina, a friend and fellow chef, we sat in the front room and started with mandarin segments filled with caramelized pork, prawn and peanuts. I then had my first ever betel leaf with prawn, pomelo and roasted coconut, and tasted my first real Thai green curry. It was a taste experience that I'll never forget. We were oohing and aahhing so much throughout the meal and dissecting the flavors that we drew the attention of the waiter, Martin, who asked if we would like to meet the chef. We said yes, and out of the kitchen came David Thompson, charming and so full of information. When he walked away from the table, I knew Darley Street was where I wanted to work.

Little did I know that the same charming man would go on to make me cry and laugh so much—not to mention what I then saw as "torture" as he booted me into (necessary) shape and the direction that led me to become the cook I am today. Other

8

such charming "torturers" include David King, Michael Voumard and Ross Lusted, to name a few. Thank you—you'll all be pleased to know I've joined the best of the "torturers" myself!

My Longrain Day

My Longrain day always starts off with a trip to China or Thaina Town, as the local Thais call it. This is a small strip of specialty produce shops in Campbell Street, near Sydney's Chinatown. The smells, the people and the friendliness can be very chaotic first thing in the morning, but I've come to love this part of my Longrain day, especially when there are new Thai vegetables or fruit around to get me thinking about new dishes. This part of the day also gives me a chance to touch and smell the fruit and vegetables, and ensures that Longrain uses the freshest range of hand-selected ingredients.

The recipes in this book are some of my favorite dishes, and a fair few of them have featured on the Longrain menu. I want to stress to all of you who attempt the recipes from this book that much of the success of each recipe relies on tasting throughout the cooking process. The art of "tasting" was never emphasized to me as a young apprentice, but I can't stress enough how important it is to taste how a dish evolves from being something quite bland to something quite amazing with the addition of fish sauce, lime juice or sugar. Tasting as you go, more than quantities and methods, is the big secret to the success of the finished dish. The strength of some herbs and spices also changes with the seasons and the water levels, so something like coriander leaves may taste stronger in, say, July than in December.

I am terrible when it comes to writing things down after or during the making of a dish—as a result, many of my best dishes have never been the same again—mainly because I've forgotten that little pinch or splash of whatever I had in front of me at the time. So sitting still with pen and paper and a computer and writing the recipes for this book has been quite a challenge.

Cooking Asian food may be a new experience for many people, but relax and enjoy the experience. As with other forms of cooking, there are always opportunities to fix things that go wrong. For example, when something is too hot, add some sugar. When something is too sour, add some salt, sugar and chili. If

something is too salty you can either rescue it by adding some lime juice or . . . throw it out and start again.

Remember when you are preparing Thai food that it is more than likely going to be eaten with rice; the dish has to be well seasoned so that it works when eaten and enjoyed as a dish in its own right and when mixed through rice. There is nothing worse than mixing a dish through rice and finding that the flavors are totally lost. Season generously.

I have no secrets. What I know, I've passed on to you in this book, including all the hints and tips that come from years of hard work in the kitchen.

The Asian Table

The Asian table is a communal table, which is also how seating is organized in the restaurant. All the main meals are designed to be shared, and to be eaten with steamed jasmine rice. Most recipes feed four unless otherwise stated.

Accompaniments are an integral part of the Asian table, which means that the individual tastes of each person can be catered for. These little dishes of tasty sauces and side dishes allow you to add your own touch. For heat, there are sliced chili rounds, perhaps in soy sauce or fish sauce. There is sugar for sweetness, and vinegar if you think a dish needs a bit more of a kick. Soy sauce adds saltiness and depth, and peanuts a nutty taste and texture. On the Thai table, an accompaniment that is always on hand is Nahm Pla Prik Dipping Sauce (page 16), a mixture of chili, fish sauce, finely sliced shallots and lime juice.

My favorite relish is a mixture of finely sliced cucumber, ginger, coriander leaves and shallots with sweet vinegar—I could eat spoonfuls of it on its own. It is a great accompaniment to a delicious yellow curry (just spoon it on top and mix it through the rice and curry) and with Egg Net Rolls (page 32).

I hope the recipes in this book will help you become more familiar with Thai food. Most make use of ingredients that are readily available from Asian grocers and supermarkets. The Basics chapter (from page 13) offers recipes for curry pastes and dressings, and methods for making flavorings such as fresh Crispy-Fried Shallots and Garlic. We've also included a glossary to explain some of the less usual ingredients and how to use them.

Sam Christie has included some food and wine matching tips. The strong flavors of chili and spicy pastes can wreak havoc with some wine, and we hope the hints will help you.

Enjoy!

—Martin Boetz

Basic

Green Chili Nahm Jim Sauce

Makes 1 cup (250 ml)

1 clove garlic, peeled
2 coriander (cilantro) roots, scraped and cleaned
¾ in (2 cm) galangal root, peeled
3 tablespoons shaved palm sugar
3 tablespoons fish sauce
1 green finger-length chili, deseeded and chopped
2 green bird's-eye chilies
½ cup (125 ml) fresh lime juice

Pound the garlic, coriander roots, chilies and galangal to a uniform paste in a mortar and pestle. Add the palm sugar and fish sauce, pour over the lime juice and mix thoroughly. The dressing should taste hot, sweet, sour and salty. Add more palm sugar if needed to make it sweeter or more fish sauce to make it more salty.

Red Chili Nahm Jim Sauce

Makes 1¼ cups (310 ml)

2 red finger-length chilies, deseeded
2 red bird's-eye chilies
2 cloves garlic, peeled
2 coriander (cilantro) roots, scraped and cleaned
1 teaspoon sea salt
⅓ cup (60 g) shaved palm sugar
¼ cup (60 ml) fish sauce
¾ cup (200 ml) fresh lime juice

Pound the chilies, garlic, coriander roots and salt to a uniform paste in a mortar and pestle. Add the palm sugar, pound, then add the fish sauce and lime juice. Taste—the flavor should be a balance of sweet, sour and salty.

Chili Jam

Makes about 1 cup (250 ml)

4 cups (1 liter) oil
2 cups finely sliced red onions
¾ cup garlic, peeled, blended or finely grind
1½ cups (30 g) dried red chilies, deseeded
½ cup (60 g) dried shrimp, soaked in warm
    water for 10 minutes, then drained
1 in (3 cm) galangal root, peeled,
    sliced and dry-roasted
½ cup (100 g) shaved palm sugar
⅓ cup (100 ml) fish sauce or 1 tablespoon
    sea salt
3 tablespoons dried tamarind pulp mixed with
    ½ cup (125 ml) hot water, mashed and
    strained to obtain the juice

Heat the oil in a wok or a heavy-based saucepan until just smoking. Fry the onions until they turn golden brown. Strain through a fine-mesh metal sieve, setting the onions aside to drain. You are using the same oil for each of the fried components of this Chili Jam, so you need to strain the oil well.

Fry the garlic until a light golden color, then remove. Fry the chilies for no more than 10 seconds as they burn quite quickly. Take them out when they turn a dark red color.

Place the dried shrimp in the oil, moving them around occasionally for about 1 minute. Take out and drain on paper towels. Reserve the oil.

Add the galangal to the fried ingredients and grind everything to a paste. You can make this into a paste in one of several ways:
• pound all the fried ingredients in a large mortar and pestle in several batches

- blend them in a food processor
- use a grinder attachment and grind the ingredients in three batches then finish by blending in a food processor. This last method gives the best result.

Place the paste in a heavy-based pot, strain the reserved oil over it and stir to combine. Heat the mixture almost to boiling point. When hot, add the palm sugar, fish sauce and tamarind juice. Stir to mix through, and remove from the heat.

The paste should have a rich, roasted, sweet, sour and salty taste. It is often used as a base to flavor other dishes. Keeps for a few months.

Chili Vinegar Dipping Sauce

A vinegar that is on the tables of most Thai eating houses as an accompaniment. It is used as a side dish to cut the sweetness of the caramel and to add some heat to the recipe for pork hock (page 122).

Makes 1 cup (250 ml)

2 red finger-length chilies, finely sliced into rounds
$^3/_4$ cup (200 ml) white rice vinegar

Combine the chilies and vinegar and mix well.

Sweet Chili Sauce

Makes 1 cup (250 ml)

1 cup red finger-length chilies, deseeded
1 cups (125 g) superfine (caster) sugar
$^1/_2$ cup (125 ml) water
$^1/_2$ cup (125 ml) white vinegar
$^1/_2$ tablespoon sea salt

Blend the chilies to a paste in a food processor. Set aside.

In a heavy-based saucepan, combine the sugar, water and vinegar. Bring to a gentle boil, add the chilies and salt. Cook for a further 5 minutes, then set aside and cool.

Keep in an airtight container or jar. Use as a dipping sauce or as a dressing with lime juice.

Sweet Soy Dressing

Makes 1$^1/_2$ cups (375 ml)

3 cloves garlic, peeled
3 red bird's-eye chilies
$^3/_4$ in (2 cm) ginger root, peeled
$^1/_2$ cup light soy sauce
$^1/_2$ cup (125 ml) thick sweet soy sauce
$^1/_2$ cup (125 ml) rice vinegar
$^1/_4$ cup (65 ml) thick yellow bean sauce
$^1/_2$ cup (65 g) superfine (caster) sugar

In a mortar and pestle, pound the garlic, chilies and ginger until a uniform paste.

Put the paste and the rest of the ingredients into a heavy-based pot. Bring to a boil and simmer for 5 minutes. Cool and store in a clip-top jar.

Sweet Soy And Ginger Dressing

Makes 2 cups (500 ml)

¾ cup (180 ml) mirin or sake
⅔ cup (150 ml) water
⅔ cup (150 ml) light soy sauce
⅓ cup (100 ml) white vinegar
4 tablespoons caster sugar
1½ in (4 cm) ginger root, peeled and chopped
4 cloves garlic, peeled and finely sliced
3 red bird's-eye chilies, sliced into fine rounds
1 teaspoon sesame oil

Bring the mirin, water, light soy sauce, vinegar and caster sugar to a boil in a heavy-based saucepan over medium heat. Add the ginger, garlic, chilies and sesame oil. Simmer lightly for 5 minutes, remove from the heat and allow to cool.

Nahm Pla Prik Dipping Sauce

Makes ½ cup (125 ml)

6 red bird's-eye chilies, sliced into rounds
1 small shallot, peeled and finely sliced
⅓ cup (100 ml) fish sauce
Juice of ½ lime

Combine all the ingredients and mix well.

Black Bean Sauce

Makes just under 1 cup (250 ml)

1⅔ cups (100 g) salted preserved black beans
¾ cup (200 ml) oil
10 cloves garlic, peeled
2 dried red chilies, deseeded
1½ in (4 cm) ginger root, peeled
1 tablespoon black Chinese vinegar
2 tablespoons superfine (caster) sugar

Rinse the black beans to remove excess salt and set aside.

Heat the oil in a heavy-based saucepan until just smoking. Blend or pound the garlic to a uni-form size (but not a paste) and fry until golden brown.

Remove the garlic by passing the oil through a wire mesh strainer. Reserve the oil, and place the garlic on paper towels to drain.

Pour the hot oil back into the pan, add the chilies and fry for 30 seconds. Remove the chilies and place on paper towels. Reserve the oil.

Place the black beans, garlic, chilies and ginger in a food processor and blend to a smooth paste. Add the reserved oil, vinegar and sugar. Pour into a clip-top jar. Keeps indefinitely.

Homemade Curry Powder

Makes ½ cup

1 tablespoon coriander seeds
1 tablespoon fennel seeds
1 teaspoon cumin seeds
1 teaspoon mace blades
2 dried bird's-eye chilies
½ teaspoon ground turmeric
1 teaspoon ground white pepper

In a bowl combine the coriander, fennel, cumin, mace and chilies. Moisten with cold water and drain immediately. (Wetting the spices helps to cook the spices evenly all the way through with-out the outside catching and burning.)

Place the wet spice in a wok or heavy-based pan. Dry-roast the spices over medium heat until fragrant and dry, 5–8 minutes, stirring constantly to ensure they do not burn. Set aside to cool before adding the turmeric and pepper.

When cool, grind the spice mixture in a spice grinder or pound in a mortar and pestle and sift through a fine sieve. Store in an airtight contain-er or a clip-top jar. This mixture keeps for 2–3 weeks before the flavors start to weaken.

GREEN CURRY PASTE

Paste
1 medium red onion, peeled and sliced
5 cloves garlic, peeled
1½ in (4 cm) galangal root, peeled
2 stalks lemongrass, tender inner part of bottom
  third only
1 teaspoon sea salt
6 coriander (cilantro) roots, scraped and cleaned
6 green finger-length chilies, deseeded
8 green bird's-eye chilies
2 tablespoons sliced Chinese keys (*krachai*)
1 in (2½ cm) turmeric root
1 tablespoon dried shrimp paste
1 tablespoon grated kaffir lime rind

Spice Mix
1½ tablespoons coriander seeds
1 tablespoon cumin seeds
1 tablespoon mace blades
1 teaspoon white peppercorns
1 tablespoon sea salt

TO MAKE THE PASTE, pound the onion, garlic, galangal and lemongrass with half the salt in a mortar and pestle until a uniform paste. Remove from the mortar and place in a food processor.

Add the coriander roots, chilies, ginger, turmeric, shrimp paste and lime rind to the mortar. Pound this to a uniform paste, then add to food processor and blend everything to a smooth paste. It should have a good green color with a hint of yellow coming from the turmeric.

TO MAKE THE SPICE MIX, wet the coriander, cumin and mace, drain and dry-roast in a small heavy-based pan or wok over medium heat for 10–15 minutes. This will give all the spices ample time to roast all the way through, and do roast them slowly for that length of time as they need to be very fragrant when done. Pound in a mortar and pestle, then grind in small batches in a spice grinder to a fine powder. Pass through a fine mesh sieve.

Stir the spices into the Paste, mix well and place in an airtight container. This Paste keeps in a refrigerator for 4–6 days or you can freeze it.

JUNGLE CURRY PASTE

Paste
1 medium red onion, peeled and sliced
5 cloves garlic, peeled
2 stalks lemongrass, tender inner part of bottom
  third only
1¼ in (3 cm) turmeric root, peeled
6 coriander (cilantro) roots, scraped and cleaned
2 tablespoons sliced Chinese keys (*krachai*)
Grated rind of 1 kaffir lime
1 tablespoon dried shrimp paste, roasted
6 green finger-length chilies, deseeded
10 green bird's-eye chilies

Spice Mix
2 tablespoons coriander seeds
1 teaspoon cumin seeds
1 teaspoon white peppercorns
1 tablespoon sea salt

TO MAKE THE PASTE, pound the onion, garlic and lemongrass in a mortar and pestle to a uniform paste. Place in a food processor. Add the rest of the ingredients to the mortar and pound to a uniform paste. Transfer to the food processor and blend everything together to a smooth paste.

TO MAKE THE SPICE MIX, wet the coriander and cumin, drain and dry-roast in a small heavy-based pan or wok over medium heat for 10 minutes. This will give all the spices ample time to roast all the way through, and do roast them slowly for that length of time as they need to be very fragrant when done. Cool, combine with the peppercorns and salt and grind in a spice grinder to a fine powder. Pass through a fine mesh sieve.

Stir the spices into the Paste, mix well and place in an airtight container. This Paste keeps in a refrigerator for 4–6 days or you can freeze it.

Peanut Curry Paste

MAKES 1 CUP

Paste
1 medium red onion, peeled and sliced
5 cloves garlic, peeled
1½ in (4 cm) galangal root, peeled
1 stalk lemongrass, tender inner part of bottom
  third only, finely sliced
2 tablespoons roasted peanuts
Grated rind of 1 kaffir lime
1 teaspoon dried shrimp paste, roasted
10 dried chilies, deseeded and soaked

Spice Mix
1 tablespoon coriander seeds
1 tablespoon cumin seeds
1 teaspoon white peppercorns
1 tablespoon sea salt

TO MAKE THE PASTE, pound the onion, garlic and
galangal in a mortar and pestle to a paste. Place
in a food processor.

Add the lemongrass, peanuts, lime rind, shrimp
paste and chilies to the mortar and pound to a
paste. Add to the food processor and blend to
form a smooth red paste.

TO MAKE THE SPICE MIX, wet the coriander and
cumin, drain and dry-roast in a small heavy-based
pan or wok over medium heat for 10 minutes.
This will give all the spices ample time to roast all
the way through, and do roast them slowly for
that length of time as they need to be very
fragrant when done. Cool, combine with the
peppercorns and salt and grind in a spice grinder
to a fine powder. Pass through a fine mesh sieve.

Stir the spices into the Paste, mix well and
place in an airtight container. This Paste keeps in
a refrigerator for 4–6 days or you can freeze it.

Red Curry Paste

MAKES 1 CUP

1 medium red onion, peeled and sliced
5 cloves garlic, peeled
4 coriander (cilantro) roots, scraped and cleaned

1½ in (4 cm) galangal root, finely sliced
1 stalk lemongrass, tender inner part of bottom
  third only, finely sliced
1 teaspoon dried shrimp, soaked in warm water
1¾ oz (50 g) smoked trout
1 tablespoon dried shrimp paste, roasted
10 dried chilies, deseeded and soaked
1 tablespoon sea salt
1 tablespoon white peppercorns, ground

Pound the onion, garlic, coriander roots and
galangal in a mortar and pestle until a uniform
paste. Place in a food processor.

Pound the remaining ingredients except the
peppercorns to a uniform paste and add to the
food processor. Blend to a smooth paste. Mix
through the pepper.

Store in an airtight container. The Paste keeps
for 4–6 days in the refrigerator. It freezes well.

Rich Red Curry Paste

MAKES ABOUT 1 CUP

1 medium onion, peeled and chopped
6 cloves garlic, peeled
1 stalk lemongrass, tender inner part of bottom
  third only
1 tablespoon sea salt
1½ in (4 cm) galangal root, peeled
6 coriander (cilantro) roots, scraped and cleaned
Grated rind of 2 kaffir limes
8 dried red chilies, deseeded and soaked
1 teaspoon dried shrimp paste, roasted
1½ teaspoons coriander seeds
1 teaspoon white peppercorns

Pound the onion, garlic and lemongrass with the
salt in a mortar and pestle to a uniform paste.
Place in a food processor.

Pound the galangal, coriander roots and kaffir
lime rind and also add to the food processor.

Add the chilies and shrimp paste to the mortar
and pound to a uniform paste. Transfer to the
food processor and blend to a smooth paste. It
should smell very fragrant and citrussy.

Wet the coriander, drain and dry-roast in a
small heavy-based pan or wok until fragrant.

Cool and add the peppercorns and grind in a spice grinder to a fine powder.

Stir the spices into the Paste and seal in an airtight container. This Paste keeps for 7 days in the refrigerator or can be frozen.

LIGHT RED CURRY PASTE

MAKES 1 CUP

5 cloves garlic, peeled
1 medium onion, partially dry-roasted
1 stalk lemongrass, tender inner part of bottom third only, finely sliced
1 in (2½ cm) galangal root, peeled and finely sliced
1 tablespoon grated kaffir lime rind
2 coriander (cilantro) roots, scraped and cleaned
4 red bird's-eye chilies
1 teaspoon sea salt
1 teaspoon dried shrimp paste, roasted
8 dried red chilies, soaked and deseeded
½ teaspoon coriander seeds
½ teaspoon cumin seeds
½ teaspoon white pepper

Pound the garlic, onion, lemongrass, galangal, kaffir lime rind, coriander roots and chilies with the salt in a mortar and pestle until a uniform paste. Place in a food processor with the shrimp paste and drained chilies. Blend to a smooth paste.

Wet the coriander and cumin, drain and dry-roast in a small pan or wok until fragrant. Cool and add the peppercorns and grind in a spice grinder to a fine powder.

Stir the spices into the Paste and seal in an airtight container. This Paste keeps for 7 days in the refrigerator or can be frozen.

MUSLIM CURRY PASTE

MAKES 1 CUP

Paste
1 medium red onion, peeled and chopped
6 cloves garlic, peeled
1½ in (4 cm) galangal root, peeled
1 stalk lemongrass, tender inner part of bottom third only, finely sliced
6 coriander (cilantro) roots, scraped and cleaned
⅓ cup (100 ml) water (optional)
10 red finger-length chilies, deseeded and soaked

Spice Mix
1½ teaspoon coriander seeds
1 teaspoon cumin seeds
1 cardamom pod
1 in (2½ cm) stick cassia or cinnamon bark
3 cloves
½ teaspoon mace blades
1 star anise pod
1 tablespoon sea salt

TO MAKE THE PASTE, dry-roast the onion, garlic, galangal, lemongrass and coriander roots in a wok or heavy-based pan until softened, slightly charred and fragrant. If the ingredients are too brown or char too quickly, add the water and cover with a lid to allow the ingredients to steam and cook all the way through. Remove from the wok when cooked through and cool. Drain the chilies, combine with the rest of the ingredients and blend to a smooth brownish red paste.

TO MAKE THE SPICE MIX, wet the spices except the salt and dry-roast in a wok or heavy-based pan over medium heat for 10–15 minutes. This will give all the spices ample time to roast all the way through, and do roast them slowly for that length of time as they need to be very fragrant when done. Pound in a mortar and pestle, then grind in small batches in a spice grinder to a fine powder.

Stir the spices into the Paste and add the salt. The Paste should be rich and brown in color and have a heavy spiced aroma. Store in an airtight container for up to a week or freeze.

19

Yellow Curry Paste

Makes 1 cup

Paste
1 medium red onion, peeled and chopped
8 cloves garlic, peeled
6 coriander (cilantro) roots, scraped and cleaned
1½ in (4 cm) turmeric root, peeled and chopped
1½ in (4 cm) ginger root, peeled and chopped
8 dried red chilies, deseeded and soaked

Spice Mix
1 tablespoon coriander seeds
1 teaspoon cumin seeds
1 teaspoon fennel seeds
½ teaspoon white peppercorns
2 tablespoons sea salt

TO MAKE THE PASTE, place the onion, garlic, coriander roots, turmeric and ginger in a heavy-based pot or wok over medium heat. Stir until colored and soft. If the ingredients are taking on too much color, add a little water to slow down the cooking process. We want the ingredients to caramelize as this is going to give the finished curry depth and added flavor. When the ingredients are soft, scrape into a large bowl and add the drained chilies. Set aside to cool, then blend in a food processor for 3–4 minutes to a smooth reddish yellow paste. If the paste is not wet enough, add a little water to help move the blades.

TO MAKE THE SPICE MIX, wet the coriander, cumin and fennel, drain and dry-roast in a small heavy-based pan or wok over medium heat for 5–8 minutes. This will give all the spices ample time to roast all the way through, and do roast them slowly for that length of time as they need to be very fragrant when done. Cool, then combine with the peppercorns and salt and grind in small batches in a spice grinder to a fine powder. Pass through a fine mesh sieve.

Stir the spices into the Paste, mix well and place in an airtight container. This Paste keeps in a refrigerator for 4–6 days or you can freeze it.

Roasted Rice Powder

Add a handful of uncooked glutinous rice grains to a dry, heated skillet. Dry-roast over moderate heat, stirring constantly until the rice turns a golden brown. Pound until fine in batches using a mortar and pestle or grind in a spice grinder until a fine powder is formed. Store in an airtight container.

Salt And Pepper Mix

Makes 1½ cups

3½ tablespoons (50 g) Sichuan peppercorns
1 teaspoon coriander seeds
1 teaspoon whole cloves
2 star anise pods
1 stick cassia or cinnamon bark
5 small dried red chilies
7 tablespoons (100 g) sea salt

Combine the Sichuan peppercorns, coriander, cloves and star anise in a bowl and cover with water. Drain.

Place the spices in a heavy-based pan and dry-roast over low heat until the spices have dried out and become fragrant. Add the chilies and continue to dry-roast, stirring constantly for another 2–3 minutes. Remove from the heat and cool.

Add the salt, mix thoroughly and grind in a spice grinder to a fine powder. Store in an airtight container.

Smoking Mix

½ cup demarara sugar
1 cup (200 g) uncooked glutinous rice
4 kaffir lime leaves
1 stick cassia or cinnamon bark, broken into pieces
2 star anise pods, broken into pieces
½ cup (25 g) jasmine tea leaves
1 pandanus leaf, shredded

Combine all the ingredients and mix well.

ROASTED CHILI, SUGAR AND SALT

SOMETHING SIMPLE TO HAVE IN THE PANTRY TO SPRINKLE OVER CRISPY-FRIED CALAMARI OR FRIED FISH WITH LIME JUICE. OR TOSS WITH CASHEWS OR PEANUTS FOR SNACKS.

MAKES 1 CUP

¾ cup (200 ml) oil
10 dried red chilies, deseeded
1 tablespoon sea salt
1 cup (125 g) superfine (caster) sugar

Heat the oil in a saucepan and fry the chilies until they turn a deep red. Remove and dry on paper towels.

In a mortar and pestle, place the chilies and salt and pound to a fine powder. Add the sugar and mix through. The mixture should have a deep red tinge to it and a hot, sweet, salty taste.

PICKLED GINGER

EARLY SUMMER IS THE BEST TIME TO PICKLE GINGER. WHEN IT'S YOUNG, IT'S EASY TO PEEL AND IS NOT TOO PEPPERY. THIS IS GREAT IN SALADS OR AS A SIDE DISH MIXED WITH CUCUMBER AND CORIANDER LEAVES.

MAKES 1 lb (500 g)

1 lbs (500 g) ginger, peeled and cut into batons
½ cup (125 ml) fish sauce
½ cup (125 ml) white rice vinegar
½ cup (65 g) superfine (caster) sugar
1 stalk lemongrass, tender inner part of bottom
    third only, bruised and sliced
2 kaffir lime leaves
1 red finger-length chili, halved

If using young ginger, wash it and place in a large bowl. If using older ginger, I tend to blanch it 2–3 times in boiling water before proceeding with the recipe.

Place the fish sauce and sugar in a heavy-based pot, bring to a boil and add the lemongrass, lime leaves and chilies. Bring to a boil and pour over the ginger.

Wash the storage jars in hot soapy water. Rinse well in hot water and place on a rack in an oven for 20 minutes at 220ºF (100ºC) to sterilize.

Place the hot ginger and pickling liquid in the jar and seal. Leave for 3 weeks before use.

ROASTED EGGPLANT AND CHILI RELISH

MAKES 1 CUP

4 long green or purple eggplants
6 red finger-length chilies
6 small shallots, unpeeled
6 cloves garlic, unpeeled
1 tomato
1 teaspoon bird's-eye chili powder
¼ cup (50 g) shaved palm sugar
3 tablespoons fish sauce or sea salt
1 tablespoon dried tamarind pulp mixed with 3
    tablespoons hot water, mashed and strained
    to obtain the juice

On a grill plate or in the oven, roast the egg-plants, chilies, shallots, garlic and tomato indi-vidually until soft and blackened on the outside, turning frequently to roast evenly.

Peel the eggplants—keep the flesh, discard the skin. Peel the shallots, garlic and tomato. Place all the ingredients in a bowl and mix well. Spoon into a mortar and pestle and pound until a uniform relish paste is achieved. Depending on the size of your mortar, you may need to do this in 2–3 batches.

Flavor with the chili powder, palm sugar, fish sauce and tamarind juice. The relish should taste hot, sweet, sour and smoky.

Eat the relish with fresh cabbage leaves or cucumber, or use as a salad base or as a sauce to accompany grilled meat or fish.

Cucumber Relish

Makes 1 lb (500 g)

3/4 cup (200 ml) rice vinegar
1 1/4 cups (150 g) superfine (caster) sugar
1 piece pickled garlic
2 coriander (cilantro) roots, scraped and cleaned
1 medium cucumber, diced
1 small shallot, peeled and finely sliced
1 in (2 1/2 cm) ginger root, peeled and very finely
    sliced
1 red finger-length chili, deseeded and very finely
    sliced
1 small bunch coriander leaves (cilantro)

Boil the vinegar with the sugar, garlic and corian-der roots. Strain and cool.

Toss the cucumber, shallot, ginger, chili and coriander leaves together, then mix into the vine-gar mixture. Place in a serving bowl.

Carrot and Daikon Mix

Makes 1 lb (500 g)

2 medium carrots, peeled and cut into matchsticks
1 small daikon radish, peeled and cut into
    matchsticks
Sweet vinegar (page 23) to cover
4 tablespoons Sweet Chili Sauce (page 15)

Mix the carrot and daikon thoroughly in a bowl and pack into a clip-top jar. Pour over enough Sweet Vinegar to cover, add the Sweet Chili Sauce and seal. Keeps for 2–3 weeks, refrig-erated.

Green Shallot Pancakes

These are great for parties or as a starter filled with roasted duck from Chinatown, beansprouts and hoisin sauce. Or fill with finely cut barbecue pork and serve with cucumber and Chili Jam.

Makes 25 small pancakes

1 cup (150 g) plain flour
1/2 cup (65 g) rice flour
1 tablespoon sea salt
1 cup (250 ml) milk
1 egg
2 green onions (scallions), finely sliced
1 teaspoon sesame oil
Oil, for frying

Combine the flours and salt in a bowl. Make a well in the center, pour in the milk and whisk until you get a thin, light batter the consistency of cream. Add the egg and stir in the green onion and sesame oil. Allow to stand in the refrigerator for 30 minutes before cooking.

Heat a non-stick pan to medium heat and wipe the pan with some oil.

Using a ladle, pour in just enough batter to cover the base of the pan. Move the pan around so that the mixture coats the base evenly, just like making a crêpe. You want a thin pancake, so it may take a few practice runs.

Cook until the top just sets, then flip over and cook the other side. Stack each pancake on a plate and cover with a kitchen towel as you go. Continue until all the mixture is used up. Do not refrigerate the pancakes if not using immedi-ately—leave them at room temperature.

Crispy-Fried Garlic or Shallots

Fried garlic lasts for about 5 days in an airtight container. I recommend doing the garlic and shallots in batches of about 1 cup (200 g) at a time. Garlic can be bought ready-peeled from Asian foodstores.

Peeled garlic cloves or shallots
Oil, for frying

Slice the garlic or shallots lengthwise. Take care to ensure that all slices are of an even thickness, or they will not cook evenly.

Heat the oil until just smoking. Test with a piece of garlic or shallot—it should sizzle gently. If it sizzles too furiously and burns almost instantly, the oil is too hot.

Add the garlic or shallots and move them around in the oil to ensure even cooking. When they reach a golden brown color, strain through a fine-mesh sieve. Toss the garlic or shallots around to remove excess oil and to aerate the chips. Drain on paper towels. Store in an air-tight container.

Sweet Vinegar

MAKES 2 CUPS (500 ML)

¾ cup (200 ml) rice vinegar
1¼ cups (150 g) superfine (caster) sugar
1 piece pickled ginger
2 coriander (cilantro) roots, scraped and cleaned

Boil the vinegar with the sugar, ginger and coriander roots. Strain and cool.

Palm Sugar Caramel

MAKES 2 CUPS (500 ML)

⅜ cup (100 ml) water
½ cup rock sugar, crushed
1 cup (200 g) shaved palm sugar
½ cup (100 g) dark palm sugar, shaved
1¼ in (3 cm) turmeric root, peeled
   and sliced
1 pandanus leaf or a few drops of pandanus
   essence

Combine the water and sugar in a heavy-based pan over medium heat. Bring to a boil and reduce for 5 minutes. Add the turmeric and pandanus leaf or essence and continue to cook for a further 5 minutes. Take off the heat and allow to cool.

Sugar Syrup

MAKES 2½ CUPS (625 ML)

½ lb (250 g) superfine (caster) sugar
2 cups (500 ml) water

Combine the sugar and water in a heavy-based saucepan over a moderate heat and stir until the sugar dissolves.

Starters

grilled scallops with peanut nahm jim sauce

GREAT AS A SNACK WITH DRINKS.

SERVES 4

8 large fresh scallops on the half-shell
Oil, for brushing
Sea salt
1 bunch coriander leaves (cilantro)
1 green onion (scallion), finely sliced
1 green finger-length chili, deseeded and very finely sliced
1 in (2½ cm) ginger root, peeled and very finely sliced

Peanut Nahm Jim Sauce
⅓ cup (50 g) roasted peanuts
½ cup (100 g) shaved palm sugar
3 tablespoons water
1 clove garlic, peeled
1 green finger-length chili, deseeded
1 green bird's-eye chili
1 coriander (cilantro) root, scraped and cleaned
1 tablespoon minced ginger
⅔ cup (150 ml) fresh lime juice
3 tablespoons fish sauce

TO MAKE THE PEANUT NAHM JIM SAUCE, place the peanuts on a small metal tray or baking pan.

Combine the palm sugar and water in a small saucepan and bring to a boil. The water will evaporate, helping the sugar to break down quickly. Let the sugar caramelize slightly, then pour it over the peanuts. Set aside to cool and harden.

Pound the garlic, chilies, coriander root and ginger in a mortar and pestle to a uniform paste. Pound the peanut toffee into the mix and combine well.

Pour over the lime juice, mix well and taste: it should be sweet, sour and nutty. Add the fish sauce to balance the flavors—it should now be sweet, sour and salty.

Brush each scallop with a little oil and season with salt.

Place the shells under a broiler or on top of a grill to heat. Once the shells are hot, place the scallops in the shells and grill for about 30 seconds on each side. Remove the shells and place on a serving plate. Spoon some Peanut Nahm Jim Sauce over each scallop.

Combine the coriander leaves, green onion, chili and ginger in a bowl. Dress with the Peanut Nahm Jim Sauce and place just enough salad for a mouthful onto each scallop. Serve immediately.

grilled scallops with crispy sweet pork and herbs

THE SWEET PORK IS CUT BY THE HOT AND SOUR DRESSING, THEN THE SWEETNESS OF THE SCALLOP COMES THROUGH—A GREAT COMBINATION OF FLAVORS AND TEXTURES.

SERVES 4

Oil for frying
8 large fresh scallops
Sea salt
8 betel leaves or soft lettuce leaves

Crispy Sweet Pork
5 oz (150 g) pork shoulder (pork neck)
6 tablespoons oil
1 star anise pod
½ in (1 cm) ginger root, peeled
1 clove garlic, peeled
1 coriander (cilantro) root, scraped and cleaned
4 white peppercorns
1 cup (200 g) shaved palm sugar
2½ tablespoons water
2½ tablespoons fish sauce

Hot and Sour Dressing
3 tablespoons lime juice
½ teaspoon ground red pepper
1½ tablespoons fish sauce

Herb Salad
½ bunch coriander leaves (cilantro)
½ bunch mint leaves
1 red finger-length chili, deseeded and very finely sliced
1 stalk lemongrass, tender inner part of bottom third only, finely sliced
2 kaffir lime leaves, very finely sliced

TO MAKE THE CRISPY SWEET PORK, place the pork in a steamer set over a saucepan of simmering water and steam, covered, for 20 minutes until cooked through. Cool, then cut into cubes.

Heat 2 cups of oil in a wok. Add the pork and shallow-fry over medium heat until crisp and golden, then drain on paper towels.

Place the star anise, ginger, garlic, coriander root and peppercorns in a mortar and pestle and pound to a uniform paste.

Heat 3 tablespoons of oil in a pan and fry the paste until fragrant. Drain away the excess oil. Add the palm sugar and water, and cook over medium heat until the sugar has caramelized slightly. Add the fish sauce and mix well. Remove from the heat and mix in the pork. Set aside until ready to use.

TO MAKE THE HOT AND SOUR DRESSING, combine all the ingredients and mix well.

Heat some oil in a non-stick pan. Season the scallops with salt and sear on both sides until golden. Remove and place on the betel or lettuce leaves. Spoon over the Crispy Sweet Pork, about 1 teaspoon per scallop. Toss the Herb Salad ingredients together, moistening with the Hot and Sour Dressing. Place a little salad on each scallop and serve.

tea-smoked oysters with cucumber and ginger salad

THESE OYSTERS MAKE EXCELLENT HORS D'OEUVRES—JUST CUT THE SALAD INGREDIENTS FINELY AND SERVE THE OYSTERS IN THEIR SHELLS WITH THE DRESSING OR IN CHINESE PORCELAIN SPOONS.

SERVES 4

12 large fresh oysters, shucked
½ medium cucumber, finely sliced lengthwise
1¼ in (3 cm) ginger root, peeled and very finely sliced
½ cup (25 g) coriander leaves (cilantro)
1 green finger-length chili, deseeded and very finely sliced
4 tablespoons Sweet Soy and Ginger Dressing (page 16)
Juice of 1 lime
Crispy-Fried Shallots (page 23)

Smoking Mix
½ cup demarara sugar
1 cup (200 g) uncooked glutinous rice
4 kaffir lime leaves
1 cassia or cinnamon bark, broken into pieces
2 star anise pods, broken into pieces
½ cup (25 g) jasmine tea leaves
1 pandanus leaf, shredded

MAKE THE SWEET SOY AND GINGER DRESSING AND CRISPY-FRIED SHALLOTS by following the recipes on pages 16 and 23.

TO MAKE THE SMOKING MIX, combine all the ingredients and mix well.

Line the bottom of a wok with foil. Place the Smoking Mix ingredients on the foil in the wok. Make sure the kitchen is well-ventilated, turn the heat to high and start to smoke the ingredients.

Line a steamer basket with a banana leaf and place the oysters on it.

Place the steamer in the smoking wok, turn off the heat and cover with the steamer lid and let the smoke infuse into the oysters for about 5 minutes. This method gives a caramelized, smoky flavor to the oysters.

Toss all the other ingredients together, add the oysters and mix well. Spoon over the dressing and squeeze in some lime juice. Put the salad on a serving plate and sprinkle with Crispy-Fried Shallots.

steamed clams with thai herbs

THIS DISH CAN BE PREPARED IN ADVANCE AND MAKES A PERFECT SNACK. SERVE WITH COLD BEER!

SERVES 4 AS PART OF A SHARED MEAL

2 lbs (1 kg) fresh clams (vongole)
2 portions Green Chili Nahm Jim Sauce
    (page 14)

Thai Herbs
1 cup (40 g) Thai basil leaves
½ cup (25 g) coriander leaves (cilantro)
2 in (5 cm) ginger root, peeled and very
    finely sliced
4 kaffir lime leaves, finely shredded
1 stalk lemongrass, tender inner part of
    bottom third only, finely sliced
1 green finger-length chili, deseeded and very
    finely sliced
1 red finger-length chili, deseeded and very
    finely sliced

MAKE THE GREEN CHILI NAHM JIM SAUCE by following the recipe on page 14.

Steam the clams until the shells open. Cool. Save any excess juices from the shellfish.

Pour the Sauce over the clams and let it mix with the shellfish juices. It will dilute a bit so don't worry if you thought the Nahm Jim was too strong to begin with.

Refrigerate the dish at this point if you are serving it later.

To serve, mix in the Thai Herbs. Toss together with the clams and serve in a deep bowl or plate.

egg net rolls with pork and shrimp

SERVES 4

4 eggs, beaten
Oil, for pan frying
1 portion Cucumber Relish (page 22)

Coconut Caramel Sauce
2 cloves garlic, peeled
3 coriander (cilantro) roots, scraped and cleaned
1 in (2½ cm) ginger root, peeled
5 white peppercorns
½ cup (100 g) shaved palm sugar
Flesh of 1 coconut, finely grated in a food
   processor
1 teaspoon dried shrimp paste, roasted and
   ground
2 teaspoons dried shrimp, blended to a powder
3 tablespoons fish sauce

3 tablespoons water
Juice of ½ lime

Filling
4 large fresh shrimp, peeled, deveined and
   sliced in half lengthwise
4 oz (100 g) lean ground pork
2 cups (100 g) beansprouts
2 kaffir lime leaves, finely shredded
1 stalk lemongrass, tender inner part of
   bottom third only, finely sliced
½ cup (25 g) coriander leaves (cilantro)
½ cup (20 g) mint leaves
1 red finger-length chili, deseeded and sliced
2 tablespoons peanuts, roasted and crushed

MAKE THE CUCUMBER RELISH by following the recipe on page 22.

Strain the eggs, then leave for a few hours to settle. This allows the proteins in the egg to break down so that it streams when you make the egg net rather than clumping together.

TO MAKE THE EGG NETS, heat some oil in a non-stick pan. Dip your fingertips in the beaten egg and drizzle the mixture over the pan in opposite directions to form a cross-hatch pattern. (This is a messy process, so cover your stove with foil before you start.) Once the egg sets, transfer to a plate. Repeat. You should be able to make 8 Egg Nets. If making ahead of time, cool and cover with plastic wrap to keep them from drying out.

TO MAKE THE COCONUT CARAMEL SAUCE, pound the garlic, coriander roots, ginger and white peppercorns to a paste in a mortar and pestle. In a heavy-based pot, add as little oil as possible and fry the paste until light brown. Add more oil if needed (it can be strained off before the sugar is added). Add the palm sugar and stir until it melts (add some hot water if necessary). Let the sugar slightly caramelize, then add the coconut, shrimp paste and floss. Bring the mixture to a light boil, add the fish sauce and water. Stir well and taste—it should be sweet and salty. Set the sauce aside and cool to room temperature.

TO MAKE THE FILLING, toss the shrimp in a hot wok in a little oil until just cooked. Remove, and cook the pork. Set aside and cool to room temperature, then mix with the rest of the Filling ingredients. Bind the Filling with the Coconut Caramel Sauce and taste, adjusting if necessary. Add a squeeze of lime juice for freshness.

To serve, place an Egg Net on a serving plate. Put the Filling on one side of the egg net and fold over. Serve individually or as part of a meal with the Cucumber Relish.

grilled shrimp with green chili dressing

KEEP THE HEADS AND TAILS OF THE SHRIMP ON FOR THIS DISH—REMOVE THE SHELL FROM THE MIDDLE SECTION ONLY.

SERVES 4

8 fresh jumbo shrimp, shelled
   and deveined
Splash of fish sauce
Crispy-Fried Shallots (page 23)

Green Chili Dressing
1 clove garlic, peeled
1 small knob galangal root, peeled
1 tablespoon Crispy-Fried Shallots (page 23)
1 green finger-length chili, deseeded
2 green bird's-eye chilies
¼ cup (50 g) shaved palm sugar
⅔ cup (150 ml) freshly squeezed lime juice
3 tablespoons fish sauce

Thai Herbs
½ cup (25 g) coriander leaves (cilantro)
½ cup (20 g) mint leaves
1 green finger-length chili, deseeded and very
   finely sliced
1 in (2½ cm) young galangal root, peeled
   and very finely sliced
2 kaffir lime leaves, very finely sliced
1 stalk lemongrass, tender inner part of
   bottom third only, finely sliced

MAKE THE CRISPY-FRIED SHALLOTS by following the recipe on page 23.
   Season the shrimp with a splash of fish sauce. Heat a grill pan and cook the shrimp until they change color and are cooked through. You can also pan-fry the shrimp. Set aside and reserve any cooking juices.
   TO MAKE THE GREEN CHILI DRESSING, pound the garlic, galangal, shallots and chilies to a uniform paste. Pound in the palm sugar, then add the lime juice and fish sauce. Taste—the Dressing should be hot, sweet, salty and sour, with the nuttiness of the shallots coming through. Set aside.
   Combine the shrimp and Thai Herbs ingredients and spoon over the Dressing. Place on a serving plate and sprinkle with more Crispy-Fried Shallots.

silken tofu with herbs and pickled ginger

A 1-IN (2½-CM) PIECE OF GINGER, VERY FINELY SLICED, ALSO WORKS IN PLACE OF THE PICKLED GINGER.

SERVES 4

7 oz (200 g) cake silken tofu, sliced
⅓ cup (100 ml) Sweet Soy and Ginger
   Dressing (page 16)
Juice of 1 lime
Crispy-Fried Shallots (page 23)

Salad
½ cup (25 g) coriander leaves (cilantro)
½ cup (20 g) mint leaves
1 red finger-length chili, deseeded and very
   finely sliced
½ medium cucumber, finely shaved into
   ribbons
2 tablespoons Pickled Ginger (page 21)
1 green onion (scallion), finely
   sliced diagonally

MAKE THE SWEET SOY AND GINGER DRESSING AND CRISPY-FRIED SHALLOTS by following
the recipes on pages 16 and 23.

MAKE THE PICKLED GINGER by following the recipe on page 21.

Place the sliced tofu on a serving plate.

Mix the Salad ingredients, combining well. Place on top of the tofu, and spoon over the
dressing and lime juice.

Sprinkle with the Crispy-Fried Shallots.

smoked trout with thai herbs

THE SMOKINESS OF THE SMOKED TROUT IN THIS DISH IS CUT WITH FRESH LIME JUICE—THE SWEET AND SOUR
FLAVORS ARE VERY LIGHT AND HERBACEOUS.

MAKES 20

4 tablespoons Red Chili Nahm Jim Sauce
    (page 14)
14 oz (400 g) smoked trout, flaked and
    skinned
2 small shallots, peeled and thinly sliced
2 red finger-length chilies, deseeded and very
    finely sliced
3 kaffir lime leaves, very finely sliced
1 cup (50 g) coriander leaves (cilantro)
20 betel leaves or soft lettuce leaves
2 oz (50 g) trout roe or salmon roe
Crispy-Fried Shallots (page 23)

Spice Paste
10 cloves garlic, peeled
2 cups oil
6 dried red chilies, deseeded
4 tablespoons dried shrimp, soaked in warm
    water for 15 minutes, then drained
2 in (5 cm) galangal root, peeled
    and finely sliced
½ cup (100 g) shaved palm sugar
⅓ cup (100 ml) fish sauce

MAKE THE RED CHILI NAHM JIM SAUCE AND CRISPY-FRIED SHALLOTS by following the
recipes on pages 14 and 23.

TO MAKE THE SPICE PASTE, blend or finely chop the garlic. Heat the oil in a wok and
deep-fry the garlic until it is golden brown. It will keep cooking after it's taken out. Strain and
drain the garlic on paper towels. Reserve the oil.

Return the oil to the wok and heat. Add the dried chilies and move them around in the oil
until they change color to a deep red, 10–12 seconds. Remove and drain.

Dry-roast the galangal in a separate pan until fragrant. Set aside to cool.

Pound the garlic, galangal, dried shrimp and chilies to a fine paste in a mortar and pestle or
blend in a food processor with ⅓ cup (100 ml) of the reserved garlic oil to help the blades move.

Remove the Paste from the blender. Place in a heavy-based saucepan on moderate heat
and cook to bring all the flavors together. Add the palm sugar and fish sauce, and stir until
the paste is amalgamated and fragrant. Do not caramelize the sugar—just allow it to melt into
the paste or it will set when cooled. Remove from the heat and cool.

To assemble, place 2 tablespoons of the cooled Spice Paste in a bowl. Add some Red Chili
Nahm Jim Sauce and stir to get a thick, sauce-like consistency.

Add the flaked fish, shallots, chilies, kaffir lime leaves and coriander leaves and gently
bring together to bind all the ingredients. Spoon onto betel or lettuce leaves, top with the
trout or salmon roe and Crispy-Fried Shallots. Repeat with the rest of the ingredients.

steamed rice noodle rolls with barbecued duck and basil

A SIMPLE LUNCH DISH OR AN ADDITION TO A LARGE DINNER BANQUET. BUY THE DUCK WHOLE FROM A CHINESE TAKEAWAY, OR USE THE SOY DUCK RECIPE ON PAGE 135.

SERVES 4

2 lbs (1 kg) fresh rice noodle sheets, uncut or you can make this on your own

3 tablespoosn hoisin sauce

1 barbecued duck, deboned and sliced, or 1 portion Soy Duck (page 135)

2 cups (100 g) beansprouts

1 bunch garlic chives

1½ in (4 cm) ginger root, cut into thin strips

1 cup (50 g) Thai basil leaves

¾ cup (200 ml) Chicken Stock (page 65)

⅔ cup (150 ml) Sweet Soy Dressing (page 15)

2 red finger-length chilies, finely sliced

1 bunch coriander leaves (cilantro)

Rice Noodle Sheets

1 cup (125 g) rice flour

3 cups (750 ml) water

½ teaspoon salt

MAKE THE RICE NOODLE SHEETS by mixing the ingredients well to form a smooth batter. Fill a steamer with water until ⅔ full and stretch a piece of cheesecloth very tightly over its top, securing it with a string. Bring the water in the steamer to a boil and brush the cheesecloth with a little oil. In a circular motion, spread a small ladle of the batter onto the cheesecloth, forming a thin, round layer of batter. Cover with a lid and steam the batter until set, 2 to 3 minutes. Remove by carefully lifting the steamed Rice Noodle Sheets from the corners with a spatula. Repeat until all the batter is used up.

MAKE THE SWEET SOY DRESSING by following the recipe on page 15.

Unfold the fresh rice noodle sheets and cut along the folds to create large rectangles. Brush the inside of the rectangles with the hoisin sauce, then add the duck, beansprouts, garlic chives, basil and ginger on the bottom third of the sheet. Roll up into tubes and place the rolls in a deep bowl, seam side down. Repeat with the remaining noodle sheets and ingredients.

Bring the Chicken Stock and Sweet Soy Dressing to a boil, then pour over the rolls so they are half covered with stock. The Sweet Soy Dressing will flavor the stock, and form the basis of a delicious sauce.

Place the bowl with the noodles into a steamer that has been set over boiling water, cover and steam for 8 minutes.

Remove the bowl from the steamer and, before serving, garnish with the sliced chili and coriander leaves.

thai fish cakes

GREAT AS AN APPETIZER OR TO SERVE WITH DRINKS. WHITE-FLESHED FISH THAT HASN'T BEEN FROZEN IS IDEAL FOR MAKING FISH CAKES.

MAKES 30

2 lbs (1 kg) fresh white fish fillets, skinned
1 egg
½ portion Red Curry Paste (page 18)
2 tablespoons superfine (caster) sugar
⅓ cup (100 ml) fish sauce

5 yard beans or 10 green beans, very finely sliced
½ cup (20 g) Thai basil leaves, finely sliced
5 kaffir lime leaves, finely sliced
Oil, for frying

MAKE THE RED CURRY PASTE by following the recipe on page 18.

MAKE THE SWEET CHILI SAUCE AND CUCUMBER RELISH by following the recipes on pages 15 and 22.

Blend the fish in a food processor until a paste consistency, about 2 minutes. Place in a large stainless steel bowl, add the egg and curry paste and mix thoroughly. Then add sugar, salt and fish sauce.

Add the beans, basil and lime leaves and mix thoroughly.

Cup your hand, pick up the mixture and slap it into the side of the bowl for 5–10 minutes to get rid of all the air bubbles.

Heat some oil in a pan and fry a small amount of the Paste to check the seasoning. It should have a salty, sweet, fragrant and hot taste. Once you're satisfied with the flavor, shape the paste into round flat cakes of about 2 tablespoons (40 g) each and refrigerate for at least 2 hours before frying.

Heat some oil in a wok until just smoking and shallow-fry the fish cakes in batches for 2 minutes on each side until golden brown.

Serve with Sweet Chili Sauce (page 15) or Cucumber Relish (page 22).

spicy pork and crab dip with crudités

Lon is a spicy dip that is good with drinks. Serve as an appetizer or a side dish with crisp, raw vegetables such as yard beans/green beans cut into lengths, baby corn, cabbage leaves, witlof, deep-fried betel leaves, crisp fish cakes and cucumber strips.

Serves 4

½ cup (100 ml) Chicken Stock (page 65)
¼ cup (50 g) ground lean pork
¾ cup (200 ml) coconut cream
1 tablespoon dried tamarind pulp mixed with 3 tablespoons hot water, mashed and strained to obtain the juice
2 tablespoons fish sauce
½ tablespoon superfine (caster) sugar
1 red finger-length chili, sliced into rounds

1 small shallot, peeled and finely sliced
1 stalk lemongrass, tender inner part of bottom third only, finely sliced
½ green mango, peeled and pitted, flesh cut into thin strips
½ cup (25 g) coriander leaves (cilantro)
½ cup (50 g) cooked crabmeat
10 mint leaves
Juice of ½ lime, to finish

Heat the Chicken Stock in a pan until boiling, add the ground pork and cook, using a spatula to break up any lumps. Now add the coconut cream and tamarind juice, fish sauce and sugar. Taste for seasoning—it should taste sweet, salty and sour.

Add the rest of the ingredients except the lime juice, fold through and remove from the heat.

Taste, and season with more sugar and fish sauce, making sure the *lon* has a good depth of flavor as it is to be served as a dip for raw vegetables.

Place in a serving bowl and stir in the lime juice.

If you like, you can serve the *lon* with some deep-fried betel leaves or shiso leaves. Just dip the leaves in a little tapioca flour and then in the batter recipe on page 114. Fry in hot oil until golden brown and crispy, about 3 minutes.

oysters with red chili nahm jim sauce

MAKES 16

16 large fresh oysters, shucked

1 portion Red Chili Nahm Jim Sauce (page 14)
Crispy-Fried Shallots (page 23)
Coriander leaves (cilantro), to garnish

MAKE THE RED CHILI NAHM JIM SAUCE AND CRISPY-FRIED SHALLOTS by following the recipes on pages 14 and 23.

Place the shucked oysters on a serving plate and spoon the Red Chili Nahm Jim Sauce over each. Garnish with Crispy-Fried Shallots and coriander leaves.

oysters poached in coconut cream with fragrant thai herbs

SERVES 4

12 large fresh oysters, shucked

1 cup (50 g) coriander leaves (cilantro)

½ cup (20 g) Thai basil leaves

1 green finger-length chili, deseeded and very finely sliced

Flesh of 1 young coconut, cut into thin strips

Juice of ½ lime

2 oz (50 g) trout roe or salmon roe

2 kaffir lime leaves, very finely sliced

Dressing

1 clove garlic, peeled

3 small bird's-eye chilies

⅔ cup (150 ml) coconut cream

½ tablespoon superfine (caster) sugar

3 tablespoons fish sauce

TO MAKE THE DRESSING, pound the garlic and chilies together. Heat the coconut cream to just below boiling point—be careful not to boil it or the cream will separate. Add the pounded garlic and chili, sugar and fish sauce. Taste: the flavor should be creamy, salty, hot and slightly sweet.

Add the oysters to the Dressing just to warm them through, quickly remove and place in a mixing bowl. Add the coriander leaves, basil, chili and coconut flesh and toss with some of the Dressing. Add a little lime juice to freshen the flavors.

Transfer the salad to plates, spoon on some trout or salmon roe and sprinkle with the kaffir lime leaves.

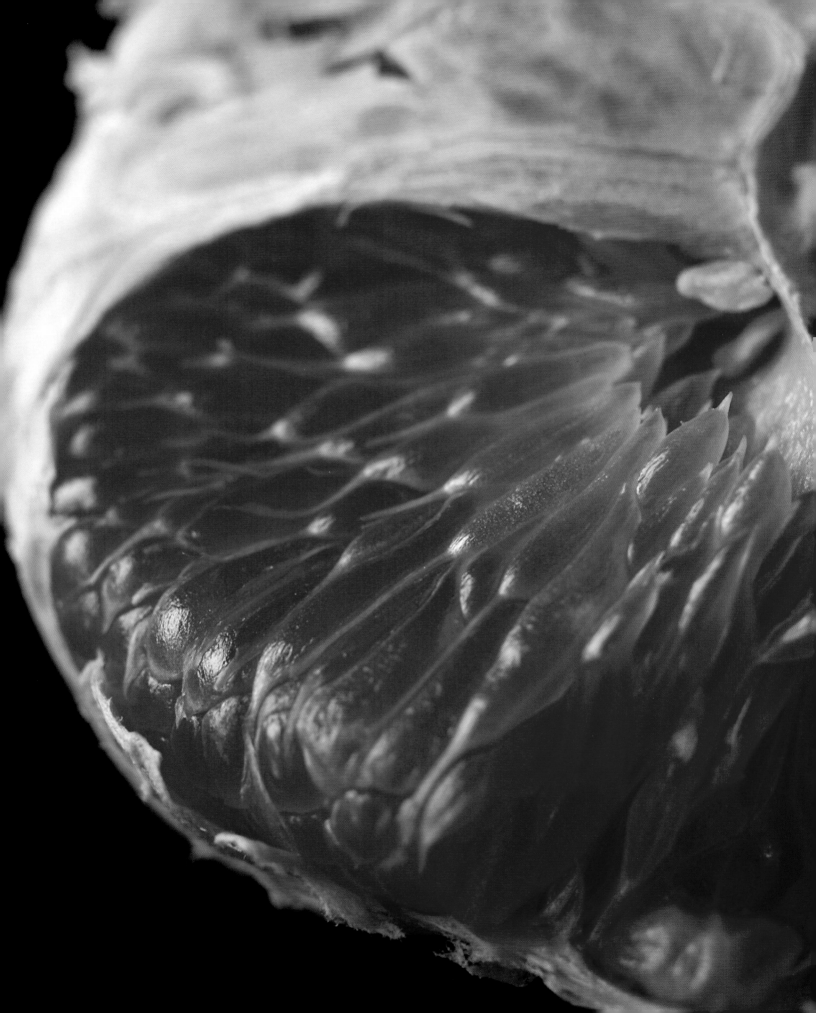

Salads

smoked trout salad
with sweet thai dressing

WE USE COLD-SMOKED OCEAN TROUT FILLET FOR THIS DISH, BUT YOU CAN ALSO USE SMOKED RIVER TROUT. THERE IS NO USE MAKING SMALL QUANTITIES OF THIS DRESSING—IT KEEPS WELL UNREFRIGERATED, AND LENDS ITSELF TO MANY USES, FOR EXAMPLE, OVER GRILLED CHICKEN OR FISH.

SERVES 4

Oil, for frying
7 oz (200 g) smoked ocean trout fillet
Crispy-Fried Shallots (page 23)
Lime wedges, to serve
Crispy-Fried Garlic (page 23)

Salad
¼ banana flower or several cabbage leaves, finely sliced
2 kaffir lime leaves, very finely sliced
10 Thai basil leaves
3–4 sprigs coriander leaves (cilantro)
1 red finger-length chili, very finely sliced
2 dried red chilies, deseeded and roasted

Sweet Thai Dressing
1½ cups (275 g) shaved palm sugar
1 stalk lemongrass, tender inner part of bottom third only, bruised
½ medium red onion, sliced
4 kaffir lime leaves
1 in (2½ cm) galangal root, sliced
4 coriander (cilantro) roots, scraped and cleaned
3 tablespoons dried tamarind pulp mixed with ½ cup (125 ml) hot water, mashed and strained to obtain the juice
⅓ cup (100 ml) fish sauce

MAKE THE CRISPY-FRIED SHALLOTS AND GARLIC by following the recipe on page 23.

Heat some oil in a pan and shallow-fry the fish on both sides until crisp. Drain on paper towels.

TO MAKE THE SWEET THAI DRESSING, melt the palm sugar in a heavy-based pot over medium heat. Add a little water to help break down the sugar. Once the sugar has melted, add the lemongrass, onion, kaffir lime leaves, galangal and coriander roots and bring to a boil. Let the sugar lightly caramelize. The ingredients will release some water into the mixture, so keep reducing until the sugar thickens again. Reduce the heat, add the tamarind juice and fish sauce, taking care as the mixture will separate. Mix well and strain, then set aside to cool. The mixture should have a honey-like consistency and taste sweet and salty. If it solidifies, return the mixture to the heat and add a little more fish sauce and tamarind juice and allow to soften again.

Toss all the Salad ingredients together. Cut or break up the fish and stir through. Toss, drizzling more sauce over the Salad to coat.

Place on a plate, garnish with the Crispy-Fried Shallots and Garlic and lime wedges.

crispy pork and cuttlefish salad

SERVES 4 AS PART OF A SHARED MEAL

7 oz (200 g) belly pork
3½ tablespoons (50 g) sea salt
⅓ cup (100 ml) vinegar
4 cups (1 liter) oil, for deep-frying
5 oz (150 g) cuttlefish, cleaned and scored
   on the underside
4 green onions (scallions), shredded
2 red finger-length chilies, very finely sliced
1½ in (4 cm) ginger root, peeled and very
   finely sliced

1 bunch coriander leaves (cilantro), washed
   and chopped
1 bunch mint leaves, washed and chopped
3 green bird's-eye chilies, finely sliced
1 shallot, peeled and finely sliced
1 stalk Chinese celery, finely sliced
3 tablespoons Sweet Soy Dressing (page 15)
Juice of 1 lime

MAKE THE SWEET SOY DRESSING by following the recipe on page 15.

Set a steamer basket over boiling water and steam the pork, covered, for 35 minutes until cooked. Cool slightly, then prick the skin all over with a fork and massage the salt and vinegar into the skin. Rub a little salt and vinegar on the other side as well. Place the pork on a cake rack with a tray underneath to catch any drippings as the pork cools. When cool, remove the pork from the rack and refrigerate for 1–2 hours until it firms (this makes the pork easier to slice).

Slice the pork into long, fine strips along the grain.

Heat the oil in a wok until just smoking and fry the pork until brown and crisp, 3–4 minutes. Drain on paper towels and set aside.

Bring a pot of water to a boil, add salt to season and blanch the cuttlefish. Once it curls up, it's done. Refresh in cold water and set aside. You can grill the cuttlefish instead of blanching if you like—rub with some thick sweet soy sauce first before grilling.

Mix the rest of the ingredients together in a bowl. Toss the crisp pork and cuttlefish with the salad and place on a serving plate.

seared salmon salad with roasted shallot and chili dressing

ONE OF MY FAVORITE SALADS—THE DRESSING HAS GREAT DEPTH OF FLAVOR FROM THE ROASTED SHALLOTS AND FRIED CHILIES.

SERVES 4 AS PART OF A SHARED MEAL

2 tablespoons oil
7 oz (200 g) salmon fillet
1 tablespoon Crispy-Fried Garlic (page 23)

Dressing
3 dried chilies, deseeded and fried
    until crisp
½ teaspoon sea salt
⅓ cup (50 g) superfine (caster) sugar
2 small shallots, roasted and peeled
⅓ cup (100 ml) freshly squeezed lime juice

Salad
1 green onion (scallion), sliced into strips
    lengthwise
½ medium cucumber, sliced into long strips
    lengthwise
1 red finger-length chili, very finely sliced
2 small shallots, roasted, peeled and halved
½ bunch coriander leaves (cilantro)
½ bunch mint leaves

MAKE THE CRISPY-FRIED GARLIC by following the recipe on page 23.

TO MAKE THE DRESSING, pound the chilies with the salt and sugar in a mortar and pestle until almost a powder. Add the shallots and pound until a uniform paste. Add the lime juice and mix well with a spoon. Check the seasoning: it should taste sweet, hot and sour with a good caramel flavor.

Heat the oil in a skillet and sear the salmon on both sides until medium rare, about 1½ minutes on each side. Take off the skin and reserve. Cut the fillet into 6 pieces.

Place the salmon in a mixing bowl and add the Salad ingredients. Bind the ingredients together gently with the Dressing.

Place the salmon skin in a pan with a little hot oil and fry for 2 minutes. Drain on paper towels.

Place the Salad onto a serving plate, spoon over a little more Dressing, garnish with the crisp salmon skin and Crispy Fried Garlic.

grilled beef salad with thai dressing

SERVE THIS SALAD WITH SOME FRESH VEGETABLES ON THE SIDE TO COOL THE MOUTH. THE ROASTED RICE POWDER IS A WORTHWHILE ADDITION—IT GIVES THE FINISHED DISH EXTRA TEXTURE AND NUTTINESS.

SERVES 4

7 oz (200 g) sirloin steak
1 tablespoon thick sweet soy sauce
1 tablespoon Roasted Rice Powder (page 20)

Salad
1 apple eggplant or long eggplant, very
   thinly sliced
1 green onion (scallion), finely sliced
½ cup (25 g) coriander leaves (cilantro)
½ cup (20 g) mint leaves
1 small shallot, peeled and finely sliced
1 red finger-length chili, deseeded and very
   finely sliced

Dressing
⅓ cup (100 ml) lime juice
1 teaspoon roasted ground red pepper
3 tablespoons fish sauce
3 bird's-eye chilies, finely sliced
2 tablespoons Sweet Chili Sauce (page 15)

MAKE THE ROASTED RICE POWDER AND SWEET CHILI SAUCE by following the recipes on pages 20 and 15.

Rub the sweet soy sauce all over the beef and grill over medium–high heat until rare, about 8 minutes. Allow to rest for 8–10 minutes.

While the meat is resting, toss all the Salad ingredients together.

Slice the beef and mix through the Salad, adding the meat juices.

TO MAKE THE DRESSING, combine all the ingredients and mix well. Taste—it should be hot, sour, salty and slightly sweet.

Pour the Dressing over the Salad and fold through to mix the flavors. Sprinkle with the Roasted Rice Powder. Serve with some raw, sliced vegetables on the side.

shredded chicken salad with coconut cream dressing

2 cups (500 ml) coconut cream
2 cups (500 ml) Chicken Stock (page 65)
10 kaffir lime leaves
2 stalks lemongrass, tender inner part of
    bottom third only, bruised and sliced
2 in (5 cm) galangal root, peeled and sliced
⅓ cup (100 ml) fish sauce
⅓ cup (100 ml)) oyster sauce
1 tablespoon superfine (caster) sugar
2 chicken breasts
Crispy-Fried Shallots (page 23)
Lime wedges, to serve

Salad
7 oz (200 g) wingbeans or yard beans/green
    beans
2 red finger-length chilies, deseeded and very
    finely sliced

½ cup (100 g) shredded fresh or dried coconut
2 small shallots, peeled and finely sliced
3 kaffir lime leaves, finely shredded
1 stalk lemongrass, tender inner part of
    bottom third only, finely sliced
½ cup (20 g) mint leaves
½ cup (25 g) coriander leaves (cilantro)
½ cup (20 g) Thai basil leaves

Dressing
⅓ cup (100 ml) reserved broth from the
    chicken
⅓ cup (100 ml) coconut cream
1 clove garlic, peeled
3 green bird's-eye chilies
3 tablespoons fish sauce
1 teaspoon superfine (caster) sugar
Juice of ½ lime

MAKE THE CRISPY-FRIED SHALLOTS by following the recipe on page 23.

Pour the coconut cream and Chicken Stock into a large, deep pot. Bring to a boil and add the kaffir lime leaves, lemongrass, galangal, fish and oyster sauces and sugar and infuse for 5 minutes.

Wash and drain the chicken, add to the simmering coconut broth and poach for 25–30 minutes over low heat. When cooked, remove the chicken and drain on a plate or rack. Strain the broth and reserve for use as a delicious soup base. You will need ⅓ cup (100 ml) of the broth for the dressing.

Shred the chicken meat with your fingers, tearing along the grain to get long thin strips.

TO MAKE THE SALAD, lightly steam or blanch the wingbeans or yard beans/green beans until just cooked. Cut into bite-sized pieces and toss with the other Salad ingredients.

TO MAKE THE DRESSING, combine the reserved broth from the chicken with the coconut cream in a saucepan and heat.

Pound the garlic and chilies to a paste. Add to the hot liquid, season with fish sauce and sugar. Do not boil—keep the mixture on a gentle simmer.

Add the chicken to the Dressing and warm through, then pour over the Salad. Toss and serve immediately. Garnish with some Crispy-Fried Shallots and lime wedges.

crisp noodle salad with chicken

I USE WAISEN RICE VERMICELLI FOR THIS DISH, WHICH IS A REINTERPRETATION OF THE FAMOUS MEE GROB. YOU CAN GARNISH WITH FINELY SHREDDED OMELET AND A WEDGE OF LIME.

SERVES 4

2 tablespoons oil
7 oz (200 g) ground chicken
5 fresh shrimp, shelled, deveined and chopped
¾ cup (150 g) shaved palm sugar
4 oz (100 g) yellow beans, mashed to a paste
3 tablespoons fish sauce
Juice of 1 mandarin

Noodles
3½ oz (100 g) rice vermicelli
1 egg, for eggwash
Oil for deep-frying

Salad
4 stalks garlic chives, cut into lengths
1 red finger-length chili, very finely sliced
Rind of ½ mandarin, cut into thin strips
1 small shallot, peeled and finely sliced
1 head pickled garlic, finely sliced
2 squares hard bean curd, diced and deep-fried
½ cup (25 g) coriander leaves (cilantro)

Soak the noodles in water (from the tap will do) for 20 minutes until soft. Drain and spread out on paper towels to absorb any excess moisture. Separate the noodles into individual strands as much as possible. Lightly brush the noodles with a little eggwash—this will make the noodles turn a golden color when cooked.

Heat the oil in a wok until just smoking. Pick up small bunches of noodles at a time, and drop them into the hot oil in batches. They should separate and cover the surface of the oil and look like a spider's web. When it finishes sizzling (about 30 seconds), remove the noodles with a Chinese spider (spatula). Drain on paper towels. Repeat with the remaining noodles.

Heat the oil in a wok and stir-fry the chicken and shrimp until cooked. Drain away any excess liquid and set aside.

In a heavy-based pan, melt the palm sugar with a little water to help break down the sugar. Allow the sugar to caramelize, then add the yellow beans and fish sauce and combine until thickened. Remove from the heat and fold through the chicken and shrimp mixture. Set aside.

When ready to serve, place the chicken in a mixing bowl and add the mandarin juice. Mix well. Toss in all the Salad ingredients and lightly mix to bind all the ingredients together. Break up the crisp noodles and toss through the Salad. Serve at once, as the noodles lose their crispness if left to sit for too long.

green papaya salad with coconut rice

A LARGE CLAY MORTAR AND PESTLE IS USED IN THAILAND FOR MAKING THIS DISH—THE PESTLE IS MADE OF WOOD, WHICH BRUISES THE INGREDIENTS WITHOUT CRUSHING THEM.

SERVES 4

2 green bird's-eye chilies
1 clove garlic, peeled
1 tablespoon shaved palm sugar
1 tablespoon dried shrimp, soaked in warm water for 10 minutes to soften, drained
1 ripe tomato, thinly sliced
1 yard bean or several green beans, cut into pieces
1 teaspoon dried tamarind pulp, mixed with 1 tablespoon hot water, mashed and strained to obtain the juice

1 tablespoon freshly squeezed lime juice
1 tablespoon fish sauce
4 tablespoons roasted peanuts, crushed
1 medium green papaya, finely shredded into threads using a mandolin
½ apple eggplant or long eggplant, sliced

Coconut Rice
1 cup (200 g) uncooked jasmine rice
1½ cups (375 ml) coconut milk

TO MAKE THE COCONUT RICE, wash the rice, cover with the coconut milk and cook as you would normal rice.

Add the chilies and garlic to a clay mortar and pestle and pound to a paste. Add the palm sugar and drained dried shrimp, lightly bruise, then add the tomato and yard or green beans. Pound and bruise; the liquid released will form a light sauce. Add the tamarind juice, lime juice and fish sauce. Taste—it should be sweet, sour and salty. If you think it's intense, remember that the green papaya is yet to be added. Add the peanuts and mix through.

Add the green papaya and eggplant and pound. With your hand and a spoon, mix to combine all the flavors in the mortar. Taste and adjust the seasoning if necessary. Spoon onto a serving plate and serve with Coconut Rice.

grilled octopus with pineapple, mint and sweet chili dressing

3 tablespoons thick sweet soy sauce
7 oz (200 g) baby octopus, cleaned and
  blanched

Dressing
⅓ cup (100 ml) lime juice
2 tablespoons dried shrimp, ground to a
  powder in a food processor or blender
½ teaspoon ground red pepper
2 tablespoons Sweet Chili Sauce (page 15)
2 green bird's-eye chilies, sliced

Salad
½ cup (100 g) cored and peeled pineapple,
  sliced into thin strips
½ cup (25 g) coriander leaves (cilantro)
½ cup (20 g) mint leaves
1 red finger-length chili, deseeded and very
  finely sliced
1 green onion (scallion), very finely sliced

Rub the thick sweet soy sauce over the octopus. Heat a grill and cook the octopus until the surface is caramelized and has a nice golden color.

TO MAKE THE DRESSING, combine all the ingredients in a bowl and mix well.

Place all the Salad ingredients in a bowl, add the warm octopus and moisten with the Dressing. Finish with more ground dried shrimp and some Crispy-Fried Shallots if you like.

shrimp and pork salad

SERVES 4

8 fresh jumbo shrimp
¾ cup (200 ml) Chicken Stock (page 65)
7 oz (200 g) lean ground pork
⅓ cup (100 ml) fish sauce
1 teaspoon superfine (caster) sugar
2 red bird's-eye chilies, dry-roasted in a
    skillet and pounded in a mortar or spice
    grinder
½ cup (25 g) coriander leaves (cilantro)

½ cup (20 g) mint leaves
2 small shallots, peeled and sliced
2 green onions (scallions), cut into small,
    fine rounds
5 sawtooth herb leaves, finely sliced
Juice of 2 limes
2 tablespoons Roasted Rice Powder (page 20)

MAKE THE ROASTED RICE POWDER by following the recipe on page 20.

Steam or poach the shrimp for about 3 minutes until the shells turn red. Remove the shells.

In a wok, heat the Chicken Stock and add the pork. Cook and break up the lumps with the spatula so that the meat is loose. Add the fish sauce, sugar and chili powder. Taste—it should be hot and salty. Add the shrimp. Remove from the heat and transfer the mixture to a stainless steel bowl. Add the herbs, lime juice and a tablespoon of the Roasted Rice Powder.

Spoon onto serving plates and sprinkle with the remaining Roasted Rice Powder.

grilled calamari and pomelo salad

THE CARAMELIZED SWEETNESS OF THE CALAMARI IS A NICE FOIL FOR THE FRESH HERBS AND CHILIES. YOU CAN ADD A QUARTER OF A BANANA FLOWER, FINELY SLICED, TO THIS SALAD, FOR EXTRA TEXTURE.

SERVES 6 AS PART OF A SHARED MEAL

7 oz (200 g) fresh calamari (squid), scored
Splash of thick sweet soy sauce
1 portion Red Chili Nahm Jim Sauce (page 14)
Crispy-Fried Shallots (page 23)

Salad
1 pomelo or 2 grapefruits, peeled and
    segmented
1 stalk lemongrass, tender inner part of
    bottom third only, finely sliced
2 kaffir lime leaves, very finely sliced
1 bunch coriander leaves (cilantro)
1 bunch mint leaves
1 red finger-length chili, deseeded and very
    finely sliced
¼ cucumber, shaved into ribbons
1 small shallot, peeled and finely sliced

MAKE THE RED CHILI NAHM JIM SAUCE AND CRISPY-FRIED SHALLOTS by following the recipes on pages 14 and 23.

Toss the calamari with the sweet soy sauce before grilling.

Heat a grill pan and cook the calamari over medium–high heat for about 3 minutes.

Place the calamari in a mixing bowl, add the Salad ingredients and half the Red Chili Nahm Jim Sauce. Toss the ingredients to mix well.

Place on a serving plate, drizzle with the remaining Nahm Jim Sauce and garnish with Crispy-Fried Shallots.

crisp roast duck and lychee salad

IF YOU ARE BUYING YOUR DUCK FROM AN ASIAN RESTAURANT, ASK FOR A SMALL CONTAINER OF DRIPPINGS FOR USE IN THE DRESSING. OR YOU CAN USE SOME MASTER STOCK (PAGE 65). YOU CAN USE CANNED LONGANS OR LYCHEES IN PLACE OF FRESH ONES—DRAIN AND RINSE THE FRUIT TO REMOVE THE EXTRA SUGAR.

SERVES 4

1 barbecued duck, deboned and cut into thin
   strips or 1 Soy Duck (page 135)
Toasted sesame seeds

Dressing
⅓ cup (100 ml) duck drippings
3 tablespoons light soy sauce
3 tablespoons dark soy sauce
2 tablespoons hoisin sauce
1 tablespoon superfine (caster) sugar
1 tablespoon black Chinese vinegar
Drop of sesame oil

Salad
2 green onions (scallions), very finely sliced
3 shallots, peeled and finely sliced
10 fresh or canned lychees, peeled and
   deseeded
1 cup (50 g) coriander leaves (cilantro)
1 medium cucumber, cut into thin strips
1½ in (4 cm) ginger root, peeled and very
   finely sliced

TO MAKE THE DRESSING, whisk all the ingredients together in a bowl and adjust the seasoning to taste. The mix of the two soys creates a rich sweetness and the black vinegar should cut through that sweetness to balance the flavors.

   TO MAKE THE SALAD, toss the sliced duck and Salad ingredients together with the Dressing. Sprinkle with toasted sesame seeds. Serve on its own or with rice.

Soups

fragrant coconut soup with shrimp and mushrooms

THE GOOD OLD FAVORITE, TOM KHA GOONG, MADE USING THE FRESHEST OF INGREDIENTS. THIS WILL MAKE YOU RESOLVE TO NEVER EAT THE TORTURED VERSIONS AGAIN!

SERVES 4

1 cup (250 ml) coconut cream
1 cup (250 ml) Chicken Stock (page 65)
4 kaffir lime leaves
2 stalks lemongrass, tender inner part of bottom third only, bruised
1½ in (4 cm) galangal root, peeled and sliced
4 small shallots, peeled and halved
4 coriander (cilantro) roots, scraped and cleaned

⅓ cup (100 ml) fish sauce
1 tablespoon superfine (caster) sugar
3 tablespoons oyster sauce
2 tablespoons Chili Jam (page 14)
8 fresh jumbo shrimp, body shell removed and deveined, heads and tails left on
6 oyster mushrooms
Juice of 2 limes
4 green bird's-eye chilies, finely sliced
Coriander leaves (cilantro), to garnish

MAKE THE CHILI JAM by following the recipe on page 14.

In a heavy-based saucepan, heat the coconut cream and stock and bring to a boil. Add the lime leaves, lemongrass, galangal, shallots and coriander roots and season with fish sauce, sugar, oyster sauce and Chili Jam. Check the seasoning—it should taste hot, salty and sweet, and the flavors of the aromatics should be coming through. Reduce the heat to a simmer, add the shrimp and mushrooms and cook for a further 4–5 minutes.

Squeeze the lime juice into serving bowls and add the chilies. Pour over the hot soup and garnish with coriander leaves.

chicken stock

MAKES 8 CUPS (2 LITERS)

3 chicken carcasses, all meat, skin and fat
   removed
10 cups (2½ liters) water

4 green onions (scallions), sliced
1 brown onion, peeled and sliced
2 pieces 1½ in (4 cm) ginger root, sliced

Wash the chicken bones thoroughly to remove any blood. Place in a large stockpot, cover with cold water and bring to a boil. As the water reaches boiling point, foam may form on the surface—skim off with a spoon to ensure a clear stock.

Once boiling point is reached, reduce the heat to a simmer, skim off any more foam and add the aromatics. Simmer for 3–5 hours over a very low heat. Strain.

The stock keeps for 2–3 days, refrigerated. Bring the stock to a boil before using.

master stock

MAKES 8 CUPS (2 LITERS)

8 cloves garlic, peeled
15 white peppercorns
Oil
½ cup (125 ml) rice wine or sherry
½ cup (125 ml) thick sweet soy sauce
1 cup (250 ml) oyster sauce

1 stick cinnamon or cassia bark
3 star anise pods
1 cup light soy sauce
8 cups (2 liters) Chicken Stock (see above)
2 pieces 1½ in (4 cm) ginger root, peeled
   and chopped

Pound the garlic and peppercorns to a paste. Fry in a little oil until it smells crisp and nutty. Deglaze with the cooking wine, then add the rest of the ingredients. Bring to a boil, and skim off any foam and excess oil. Simmer for 20 minutes, then strain, discarding all the solids. You can now use the stock to cook your choice of meat or poultry.

Strain the stock after each use and refresh with more ginger and spices each time you use it. I find that the stock can get very strong after several uses, so feel free to start your stock from scratch again.

duck and winter melon soup

FOR BETTER FLAVOR, MAKE THIS SOUP THE DAY BEFORE IT IS SERVED. LEAVE THE SOUP TO SETTLE SO THAT
THE FAT FLOATS TO THE TOP, SOLIDIFIES AND SEALS IN THE SOUP. BEFORE REHEATING, SKIM OFF THE FILM OF
SOLIDIFIED FAT.

SERVES 6

4 duck legs (marylands), trimmed of excess
   fat
1 small winter melon, peeled and cut into
   bite-sized pieces
1 preserved lime, halved
10 dried black Chinese mushrooms, soaked
   and stems discarded
Very finely sliced fresh ginger
Garlic chives

Soup
5 cloves garlic, peeled
4 coriander (cilantro) roots, scraped and cleaned
1½ in (4 cm) ginger root, peeled
8 white peppercorns
1 small red onion, peeled and sliced
⅓ cup (100 ml) oil
⅓ cup (100 ml)) rice wine or sherry
⅜ cup (60 g) rock sugar, pounded
⅔ cup (150 ml) oyster sauce
⅓ cup (100 ml) light soy sauce
6 cups (1½ liters) Chicken Stock (page 65)

TO MAKE THE SOUP, pound the garlic, coriander roots, ginger, peppercorns and onion in a
mortar and pestle until well combined and a uniform paste.

Heat the oil in a heavy-based pot. Add the paste and fry until it smells
crisp and nutty. Drain off the excess oil and deglaze the pot with the rice wine
or sherry. Add the rock sugar, oyster sauce and soy sauce and cover with the
Chicken Stock. Bring to a boil and skim. Strain the stock and keep warm.

Set a large steamer over boiling water. In a large bowl that will fit into
the steamer, place the duck pieces, winter melon, preserved lime and
mushrooms. Place the bowl in the steamer, then pour the strained stock
almost to the top of the bowl. Cover with a layer of baking paper, then with
foil. Steam the Soup for 1½ hours, checking the steamer's water level
throughout, refilling with boiling water as necessary.

When done, take the ingredients out of the steamer and check that the
duck is cooked through. The meat should fall easily off the bone and the
winter melon should be almost translucent. Taste and adjust the seasoning
if necessary.

To serve, ladle the Soup, duck and winter melon into bowls. Top each with ginger
and garlic chives. Serve hot.

chicken rice noodle soup

IF POSSIBLE, BUY THE NOODLES FRESH AS A WHOLE SHEET AND CUT IT WHEN YOU NEED IT. THIS WAY, THE NOODLES WON'T DRY OUT AND YOU CAN HAVE THEM IN YOUR PREFERRED WIDTH.

SERVES 4

1¼ cups (300 ml) Chicken Stock (page 65)
⅓ cup (100 ml) Sweet Soy Dressing (page 15)
1 in (2½ cm) ginger root, peeled and very finely sliced
2 small shallots, peeled and finely sliced
1 chicken breast, sliced into thin strips
2 pieces Chinese broccoli (*kailan*), cut into bite-sized pieces

1 lb (500 g) fresh Asian rice noodles, or 8 oz (250 g) dried rice stick noodles, soaked in boiling water for 10 minutes and drained
1 red finger-length chili, finely sliced into rounds
1 bunch coriander leaves (cilantro)
1 cup (2 oz/50 g) beansprouts
Coriander leaves (cilantro), to garnish

MAKE THE SWEET SOY DRESSING by following the recipe on page 15.

Place the stock and Sweet Soy Dressing in a saucepan and bring to a boil. Lower the heat to a simmer, taste for seasoning and add more Sweet Soy Dressing if it tastes too bland.

Add the ginger and shallots. Add the chicken and broccoli and simmer for 3–4 minutes.

In deep soup bowls, place the cut noodles, chili and coriander leaves and pour over the hot soup. Garnish the soup with beansprouts and more coriander leaves and serve. If you like, squeeze in the juice of ½ lime for extra freshness.

roast duck and black mushroom wonton soup

MAKE THIS THE DAY YOU WISH TO SERVE IT. THE BROTH SHOULD BE CLEAN-TASTING, WITH A SLIGHT GINGER AND GREEN ONION FLAVOR. YOU CAN BUY THE DUCK READY-ROASTED FROM AN ASIAN RESTAURANT, OR MAKE YOUR OWN. SHREDDED CHINESE BROCCOLI CAN BE MIXED THROUGH THE SOUP FOR ADDED TEXTURE.

SERVES 4

Wontons

½ barbecued duck, deboned

6 dried black Chinese mushrooms, soaked
   and stems discarded

2 green onions (scallions), minced

1 in (2½ cm) ginger root, peeled and very
   finely sliced

1 tablespoon hoisin sauce

½ tablespoon oyster sauce

1 packet wonton skins

Broth

2 cups (500 ml) Chicken Stock (page 65)

⅓ cup (100 ml) light soy sauce

2 tablespoons oyster sauce

½ teaspoon ground white pepper

⅓ cup (100 ml) thick sweet soy sauce

1 in (2½ cm) ginger root, peeled and very
   finely sliced

2 green onions (scallions), cut into lengths

2 tablespoons Crispy-Fried Garlic (page 23)

MAKE THE CRISPY-FRIED GARLIC by following the recipe on page 23.

TO MAKE THE WONTONS, grind the duck meat and skin finely in a food processor. Do the same with the mushroom caps. Toss in the green onions and ginger and combine. Add the hoisin and oyster sauces and mix well. The mixture should be thick and dry.

Fill the wonton skins with 1 teaspoon filling per Wonton. Place the filling in the middle of the wonton skin and gather the edges together at the top. Pinch and twist to seal the top, dabbing a bit of water inside if necessary. Repeat with the rest of the skins and Wonton mixture. Refrigerate for at least an hour before cooking.

TO MAKE THE BROTH, bring the stock, soy sauce, oyster sauce, pepper and sweet soy sauce to a boil in a saucepan. Add the ginger and green onions. Add the Wontons, and once they float to the top, take the saucepan off the heat.

Ladle the soup and Wontons into serving bowls and garnish with the Crispy-Fried Garlic.

Curries

curry pastes

The intensity and taste of certain ingredients changes with the seasons, so the recipes in this chapter are not strict guides. Go by taste—a batch of coriander leaves, for example, may taste stronger one week and be gentler the next.

Most paste quantities can safely be doubled and frozen. Frozen pastes should be used on the day of thawing for best results.

The easiest way to blend pastes at home is to first pound the ingredients in a mortar and pestle to a uniform paste. Then add them to a food processor or blender. Breaking down the fibers will save the machine from overwork, and pounding them first reduces the need to add extra water to help the blender move as the natural moisture from the ingredients has already been released.

The longer a fresh paste is kept, the more the flavors dissipate, so if possible use within 3 days.

In most dishes, you will have to cook out the curry paste, by which I mean frying the curry paste in coconut cream or oil until it no longer smells raw—no garlic or onion aromas. The cooked paste should smell nutty, and of caramelized flavors.

When using coconut cream from a can or pack, it tends to be very thick, so dilute with stock.

fresh coconut milk

Freshly squeezed coconut milk is troublesome to make, but has a wonderful creamy fresh consistency that cannot be matched using canned or packed coconut milk. Purchase coconuts that are heavy and have a lot of juice in them—the juice is wonderful to drink with ice.

1 Crack the coconut open and drain the juice.

2 Set each coconut half over a "rabbit" grater, if you have one, and grate the flesh.

3 If you don't have one, break the shell into smaller pieces by turning it over on a firm surface and knocking it with a mallet. Remove the flesh from the shell and peel the brown skin using a vegetable peeler. Grate the flesh in a blender or food processor, adding a bit of water to help the blades turn.

4 Add about 1 cup (250 ml) hot water to the grated flesh.

5 Allow the grated flesh to steep for a little while, then mash it with your hand.

6 Place small handfuls of the grated coconut in some muslin or cheesecloth.

7 Squeeze the milk into a glass or ceramic bowl.

8 Allow to settle. The "coconut cream" will rise to the top; the rest is "coconut milk".

green curry shrimp with basil

THE PORK FROM THE RECIPE FOR GRILLED PORK PINEAPPLE CURRY (PAGE 81) CAN ALSO BE USED IN THIS RECIPE IN PLACE OF THE SHRIMP.

SERVES 4

⅔ cup (150 ml) fresh coconut cream or
   ⅓ cup (100 ml) oil
3 tablespoons Green Curry Paste (page 17)
4 kaffir lime leaves
1½ cups (about 6) pea eggplants (optional)
⅓ cup (100 ml) fish sauce
½ cup (100 g) shaved palm sugar
1¼ cups (300 ml) coconut milk

1 apple eggplant or long eggplant, sliced
2 green finger-length chilies, deseeded and
   sliced
⅓ cup (50 g) bamboo shoot, sliced
3 baby corns, halved
6 large fresh jumbo shrimp, shelled and
   deveined, heads and tails left on
½ cup (20 g) Thai basil leaves

MAKE THE GREEN CURRY PASTE by following the recipe on page 17.

Heat a heavy-based pan and add the coconut cream or oil. If using the coconut cream, keep cooking and stirring until it separates before you add the curry paste. If using the oil, fry the paste until fragrant and the oil is released.

Add the lime leaves and eggplants (if using) and stir into the paste. Add the fish sauce and palm sugar, moisten with coconut milk and bring to a boil. Taste for seasoning—the mixture should be hot, salty and slightly sweet. Add more seasoning at this point if needed.

Add the apple eggplant, chilies, bamboo shoot, corn and shrimp. Reduce the heat to a simmer and continue to cook for 3 minutes. Fold or stir through the basil, remove from the heat and spoon into a serving bowl. Serve with steamed jasmine rice.

fish curry with coconut and green beans

THIS IS MY INTERPRETATION OF AN INDONESIAN CURRY, WITH MORE AROMATICS ADDED TO GIVE IT MORE FLAVOR. YOU CAN POACH THE FISH IN THE CURRY MIXTURE IF YOU DO NOT WISH TO FRY IT. THIS CURRY WORKS WELL WITH COD OR KINGFISH OR ANY OTHER LIGHT FISH.

SERVES 4 AS PART OF A SHARED MEAL

1/3 cup (100 ml) oil
3 tablespoons fish sauce
1 tablespoon superfine (caster) sugar
2 cups (500 ml) coconut milk
1 stalk lemongrass, tender inner part of bottom third only, sliced
4 slices galangal root
4–5 kaffir lime leaves
2 red finger-length chilies, deseeded and halved
3 pieces baby corns, halved
2 yard beans or 2 cups (200 g) green beans, cut into lengths
Oil for deep-frying
7 oz (200 g) white-fleshed fish fillets
Coriander leaves (cilantro), to garnish
Kaffir lime leaves, very finely sliced
3 tablespoons coconut cream

Chili Paste
4 small shallots, peeled and sliced
3 dried red chilies, soaked
4 kaffir lime leaves

TO MAKE THE CHILI PASTE, blend all the ingredients together in a food processor until a uniform paste is achieved.

Heat the oil in a wok and fry the Paste until fragrant, about 5 minutes, stirring continuously so it doesn't burn.

Add the fish sauce and sugar and stir in. Add the coconut milk and bring to a boil. Add the lemongrass, galangal and kaffir lime leaves. Let these infuse at a gentle simmer for about 3 minutes.

Add the chilies, baby corns and beans.

Meanwhile, heat some oil in a wok until smoking and deep-fry the fish until golden brown and crisp. Remove and drain.

Break up the fish into bite-sized pieces and place in a serving bowl.

Taste and season the curry mixture with extra fish sauce and sugar if needed. Pour the sauce over the fish, sprinkle with coriander leaves and kaffir lime leaves and the extra coconut cream.

dry red curry fish

If you cannot find pork fatback, use oil instead. The pork fatback gives the paste a depth of flavor. Try it with and without and see what you think—pork fatback wasn't my choice until I tasted the difference!

Makes 4 individual portions or 2 large share portions

7 oz (200 g) ground pork fatback or bacon fat
⅓ cup (100 ml) water
1 teaspoon sea salt
2 tablespoons Red Curry Paste (page 18)
1 tablespoon sliced Chinese keys (*krachai*)
3 kaffir lime leaves, torn
1 red finger-length chili, deseeded and sliced
1 tablespoon shaved palm sugar
3 tablespoons fish sauce
1 tablespoon oyster sauce
3 tablespoons Chicken Stock (page 65) or water
7 oz (200 g) white-fleshed fish fillet, cut into chunks
1 stalk fresh green peppercorns (optional)
2 yard beans or 2 cups (200 g) green beans, cut into lengths
1 apple eggplant or long eggplant, cut into wedges
1 cup (40 g) holy basil leaves
Oil
Kaffir lime leaf, very finely sliced

MAKE THE RED CURRY PASTE by following the recipe on page 18.

Combine the pork, water and salt in a pan and bring to a boil. As the water evaporates, the pork fatback will start to melt. Stir occasionally as the water evaporates. The fat should run clear, with some fat particles starting to look like deep-fried crisp bits. At this stage the pork fatback is ready to be strained.

Place a pan on a stove, add the pork fatback and heat. Add the Curry Paste and cook until it smells fragrant, 2–3 minutes. Add the sliced Chinese keys, kaffir lime leaves, chili, palm sugar, fish sauce, oyster sauce and stock. Try not to scorch the paste; if it is too hot, lower the heat and add a little more stock. Check the seasoning for a hot, salty and sweet taste.

Add the fish and peppercorns, if using, and cook for 3–4 minutes, then add the beans, eggplant and half the basil.

Heat some oil in a wok and fry the remaining basil until just crispy and dark green (but not burned). Drain on paper towels.

Spoon the curry onto a serving dish and garnish with the fried basil and finely sliced lime leaves. Serve with rice.

red curry duck

⅓ cup (100 ml) oil

3 tablespoons Light Red Curry Paste (page 19)

5 kaffir lime leaves

½ cup (100 g) shaved palm sugar

⅔ cup (150 ml) fish sauce

1 teaspoon dried tamarind pulp mixed with 1 tablespoon hot water, mashed and strained to obtain the juice

1 kaffir lime, halved

4 red finger-length chilies, deseeded and roughly chopped

3 stalks Asian watercress, cut into lengths

Kaffir lime leaf, very finely sliced, to garnish

Braised Duck

1 fresh duck (3 lbs/1½ kg), halved

4 cups (1 liter) coconut milk

4 cups (1 liter) Chicken Stock (page 65)

1 stalk lemongrass, tender inner part of bottom third only, sliced

5 kaffir lime leaves, torn

1½ in (4 cm) galangal root, peeled and sliced

⅔ cup (150 ml) fish sauce

TO MAKE THE BRAISED DUCK, preheat the oven to 350°F (180°C). Rinse and clean the duck and remove any excess fat.

In a deep heavy-based casserole pot with lid, bring the coconut milk and Chicken Stock to a boil. Add the lemongrass, lime leaves, galangal and fish sauce, then add the duck and ladle some stock over the duck to scald it. Cover and place in the oven for 1½ hours or until the duck is cooked.

MAKE THE LIGHT RED CURRY PASTE by following the recipe on page 19.

When the duck is done, remove it from the stock and allow it to rest on a wire rack. Strain the stock and reserve 2 cups (500 ml) for use in the curry. Allow the stock to settle and skim the fat off the top.

Heat the oil in a heavy-based pan and fry the curry paste and the lime leaves until fragrant. Add the palm sugar and fish sauce. When the sugar dissolves and caramelizes slightly, add the reserved 2 cups (250 ml) braising liquid and tamarind juice, and bring to a boil.

Check the seasoning—it should taste sweet, salty, sour and hot. Lower the heat and simmer.

Cut the duck down the back bone and remove the ribcage with your fingers. It should come away easily from the flesh if the duck has been braised for long enough. Discard the bone and cut each duck half into 6 serving pieces, giving 12 altogether. Add the duck to the curry with the kaffir lime and chili pieces and simmer for a further 5 minutes.

Add the watercress and simmer for a further 5 minutes, then spoon into serving dishes.

Garnish with kaffir lime leaves, and serve with steamed jasmine rice.

grilled beef curry with peanuts

SERVES 4

⅔ cup (150 ml) fresh coconut cream or
⅓ cup (100 ml) oil
3 tablespoons Peanut Curry Paste (page 18)
½ cup (100 g) shaved palm sugar
⅓ cup (100 ml) fish sauce
1¼ cups (300 ml) coconut milk
2 red finger-length chilies, deseeded and
halved

3 kaffir lime leaves, very finely sliced
2 teaspoons roasted peanuts, crushed
7 oz (200 g) rump steak or sirloin
½ cup (20 g) Thai basil leaves
Extra coconut cream, to garnish

MAKE THE PEANUT CURRY PASTE by following the recipes on page 18.

Heat a heavy-based pan and add the coconut cream or oil. If using coconut cream, keep cooking and stirring until it separates before you add the Curry Paste. If using the oil, fry the paste until fragrant and the oil is released.

Add the palm sugar, fish sauce and coconut milk, and bring to a boil. Add the chilies, lime leaves and 1 teaspoon of the peanuts. Simmer until a small film of oil forms on the surface of the mixture. Set aside.

Grill or barbecue the beef over medium–high heat for 5 minutes on each side for medium rare (more if you want the meat more well done), then allow it to rest in a warm place for 10 minutes.

Return the curry sauce to a moderate heat and add half the basil.

Slice the beef and place on a serving plate.

Add the beef juices to the curry sauce, then spoon over the beef. Garnish with the remaining peanuts, basil and a splash of coconut cream. Serve with steamed rice.

grilled pork pineapple curry

SEAFOOD WORKS WELL IN PLACE OF THE PORK; TRY THIS CURRY WITH MUSSELS.

SERVES 4

⅔ cup (150 ml) fresh coconut cream or
  ⅓ cup (100 ml) oil
3 tablespoons Red Curry Paste (page 18)
½ cup (100 g) shaved palm sugar
⅓ cup (100 ml) fish sauce
1 cup (250 ml) coconut milk
3 red finger-length chilies, halved and
  deseeded

7 oz (200 g) pork shoulder (pork neck)
1 teaspoon fennel seeds
1 teaspoon sea salt
¼ fresh pineapple, peeled and cored and
  chopped into bite-sized chunks
Thai basil leaves, to finish

MAKE THE RED CURRY PASTE by following the recipe on page 18.

Heat a heavy-based pan and add the coconut cream or oil. If using coconut cream, keep cooking and stirring until it separates before you add the Curry Paste. If using the oil, fry the paste until fragrant and the oil is released.

Add the palm sugar and fish sauce, and stir until the sugar dissolves. Add the coconut milk and bring the mixture to a boil, then lower the heat to a simmer. Add the chilies and lower the heat.

Rub the pork with the fennel seeds and salt. Grill the pork on each side for 5 minutes using medium–high heat. Remove from the heat and allow to rest for 10 minutes.

Bring the curry back to a simmer and add the pineapple chunks.

Slice the pork thinly and add to the curry. Stir to combine and add the basil. Spoon into serving bowls and serve.

deep-fried snapper with rich red curry

GRILLED SHELLFISH SUCH AS CRAYFISH, SCALLOPS OR SHRIMP ARE ALSO DELICIOUS WITH THIS CURRY.

SERVES 4

⅔ cup (150 ml) fresh coconut cream or
⅓ cup (100 ml) oil
3 tablespoons Red Curry Paste (page 18)
⅓ cup (100 ml) fish sauce
½ cup (100 g) shaved palm sugar
1⅔ cups (400 ml) coconut milk
4 kaffir lime leaves
2 red finger-length chilies, deseeded and
sliced into uneven lengths

4 cups (1 liter) oil, for deep-frying
1 whole snapper or other light fish about 2
lbs (1 kg), or 1½ lbs (700 g) fish fillets
with skin on
⅓ cup (100 ml) fish sauce
½ cup (20 g) Thai basil leaves
Red finger-length chilies, very finely sliced

MAKE THE RED CURRY PASTE by following the recipe on page 18.

Heat a heavy-based pan and add the coconut cream or oil. If using coconut cream, keep cooking and stirring until it separates before you add the Curry Paste. If using the oil, fry the paste until fragrant and the oil is released.

At this point, season with fish sauce and palm sugar, stirring constantly until the sugar has dissolved into the paste.

Moisten with the coconut milk and bring to a boil. Add the kaffir lime leaves and chilies and taste for seasoning. Reduce the heat and simmer until thickened, about 5 minutes. Keep simmering on low heat, stirring from time to time to prevent scorching. Taste and check for seasoning, adjusting as necessary.

Meanwhile, heat the oil in a wok until just smoking.

Clean the fish and score on both sides, and douse with fish sauce. If using fillets, rub with fish sauce. Lower the fish into the oil and fry until golden brown. Drain the fish and place on a serving plate.

The curry sauce should now be quite thick, with a small film of oil on the top. Bring it back to a simmer, add the basil, reserving a small handful for garnish.

Spoon the curry sauce over the fish and garnish with the remaining basil leaves and some chili. A spoonful of coconut cream is also a good garnish, adding richness to the dish.

light red beef curry

Any cut of beef may be used for this curry, such as tender beef chuck, beef shin or oxtail. You will need to reserve the braising juices for the curry. This is great served with fresh rice noodles or jasmine rice.

Serves 4

1 lb (500 g) braising beef
3 cups (750 ml) coconut milk
1 stalk lemongrass, tender inner part of
    bottom third only, bruised
2 kaffir lime leaves
1¼ in (3 cm) galangal root, peeled and sliced
½ cup (100 g) shaved palm sugar
⅓ cup (100 ml) fish sauce
⅓ cup (100 ml) oyster sauce

Curry
1 cup (250 ml) coconut cream
3 tablespoons Red Curry Paste (page 18)
½ cup (100 g) shaved palm sugar
⅓ cup (100 ml) fish sauce
5 kaffir lime leaves
4 red finger-length chilies, halved, deseeded
    and very finely sliced
½ cup (20 g) Thai basil leaves
3 tablespoons light soy sauce
4 oz (100 g) rice noodles, cut into strips
Thai basil leaves, to garnish
Fresh red finger-length chilies, very finely
    sliced, to garnish

In a hot pan, sear the beef until brown on all sides. Place in a deep baking dish and set aside.

Combine the coconut milk, lemongrass, lime leaves, galangal, palm sugar, fish and oyster sauces in a large saucepan. Bring to a boil and pour over the beef. If there is leftover liquid, reserve for a later use. Cover the braising dish with a lid or seal with baking paper and foil. (I always put baking paper on first so that the foil does not react with the sauce.) Braise for about 2 hours over low heat.

When done, remove the meat from the juices, set aside to cool, then refrigerate for 2–3 hours. Reserve 1¼ cups (300 ml) of the braising liquid.

To make the Curry, prepare the Red Curry Paste by following the recipe on page 18. Heat the coconut cream in a heavy-based pan until it separates. Add the Curry Paste and fry until fragrant, about 5 minutes. Add the palm sugar and fish sauce. When the sugar dissolves, add the reserved beef braising liquid and bring to a boil.

Take the beef out of the refrigerator—the meat becomes extremely soft when cooked, and refrigeration helps to firm the meat, making it easier to cut. Slice into ½ in (1 cm) pieces.

Add the lime leaves and the beef to the curry. Simmer for 4–5 minutes with the lid on, then add the chili, basil and soy sauce. The curry should be rich in flavor from the meat stock, and taste salty and sweet. Add the rice noodles and let them soften in the liquid.

Spoon into serving bowls, and sprinkle with extra basil and chili.

muslim curry chicken

SERVES 4

¾ cup (200 ml) fresh coconut cream or
⅓ cup (100 ml) oil
3 tablespoons Muslim Curry Paste
(page 19)
1 star anise pod
1 in (2½ cm) cassia or cinnamon bark
2 bay leaves
2 cardamom pods
6 chicken drumsticks, halved
Splash of fish sauce
4 cups (1 liter) oil, for deep-frying

4 medium potatoes, peeled and halved
6 small pickling onions, peeled
1 cup (250 ml) Chicken Stock (page 65)
1 cup (250 ml) coconut cream
½ cup (100 g) shaved palm sugar
⅓ cup (100 ml) fish sauce
1 tablespoon dried tamarind pulp mixed with
2 tablespoons hot water, mashed and
strained to obtain the juice
2 tablespoons roasted peanuts, crushed
Coriander leaves (cilantro), to garnish

MAKE THE MUSLIM CURRY PASTE by following the recipe on page 19.

Heat a heavy-based pan and add the coconut cream or oil. If using coconut cream, keep cooking and stirring until it separates before you add the Curry Paste with the star anise, cassia or cinnamon bark, bay leaves and cardamom. If using the oil, fry the paste with the star anise, cassia or cinnamon bark, bay leaves and cardamom until fragrant and the oil is released. Set aside.

Toss the chicken with a splash of fish sauce.

Heat the oil in a wok until smoking and deep-fry the chicken pieces until golden brown. Remove and drain.

In the same oil, fry the potatoes and onions until golden brown. Remove and drain.

Combine the stock and coconut cream in a heavy-based pot and bring to a boil. Add the chicken and simmer until cooked, 35–40 minutes. Add the potatoes and onions and allow to cook through, but not completely as they will be cooked in the curry as well. Strain the liquid, reserving the potatoes, onions and chicken and about half the stock.

Place the Curry Paste mixture back on the heat and moisten with the reserved stock base. Place the chicken, potatoes and onions in the curry, add the palm sugar and fish sauce, and simmer.

Add the tamarind juice, stir through and taste for seasoning—it should be rich, spicy, sweet and salty.

Spoon into a serving bowl and serve topped with peanuts and coriander leaves.

spiced curry chicken

SERVES 4

6 cups (1½ liters) coconut milk
1 stalk lemongrass, tender inner part of
    bottom third only, bruised
6 coriander (cilantro) roots, scraped and
    cleaned
⅓ cup (100 ml) fish sauce
½ cup (100 g) shaved palm sugar
1 spring chicken (about 1 lb/500 g), cut in
    half
⅓ cup (100 ml) fish sauce
1 large red bell pepper, roasted and peeled
⅓ cup (50 g) peanuts, roasted and crushed
Juice of ½ mandarin orange
Fried peanuts, coarsely crushed, to garnish
1 bunch coriander leaves (cilantro)
1 tablespoon coconut cream, to dress

Curry Paste
8–12 dried chilies, deseeded
1½ cups sliced red onions
1 cup peeled garlic cloves
2 stalks lemongrass, tender inner part of
    bottom third only, finely sliced
6 coriander (cilantro) roots, scraped and cleaned
1½ in (4 cm) galangal root, peeled and finely
    sliced
2 teaspoons dried shrimp paste, roasted
1 teaspoon sea salt
1 tablespoon coriander seeds
1 tablespoon mace blades
1 teaspoon cumin seeds
3 cardamom pods
3 cloves
1 teaspoon white peppercorns

Bring the coconut milk to a boil in a large heavy-based pot. Add the lemongrass, coriander roots, fish sauce and palm sugar. Wash the chicken and place in the coconut milk. Bring to a boil, lower the heat and poach for 25 minutes. Remove the chicken and reserve 1¼ cups (300 ml) of the braising liquid. Allow the chicken to cool. Remove the center bones.

TO MAKE THE CURRY PASTE, first soak the dried chilies in warm water for about 10 minutes.

Place a wok over medium heat and dry-roast the onions and garlic, adding a little water to prevent burning. When slightly colored, after 5–10 minutes, add the lemongrass, coriander roots and galangal. Cover the wok to help the cooking process, stirring occasionally until the garlic has softened and cooked through. Add the drained chilies, shrimp paste and salt to the wok and stir well to combine. Take off the heat.

In another wok or pan, roast the coriander, mace, cumin, cardamom and cloves until fragrant. Combine with the peppercorns and grind to a fine powder.

Blend all the cooked Curry Paste ingredients in a food processor to a fine paste, then add the ground spices.

Heat a little oil in a pan and fry the Curry Paste for 10–12 minutes until fragrant and the paste smells cooked. Season with palm sugar and fish sauce, and add the reserved braising liquid. Bring to a boil, add the chicken and bell pepper. Simmer for 5–10 minutes, then add the peanuts and mandarin juice. Transfer to a serving platter and garnish with extra fried peanuts, coriander leaves and a little coconut cream.

yellow curry chicken
with sweet potato

1 cup (250 ml) coconut cream

4 tablespoons Yellow Curry Paste (page 20)

4 chicken legs, quartered, skin on

½ cup (100 g) shaved palm sugar

⅓ cup (100 ml) fish sauce

1⅔ cups (400 ml) coconut milk

2 medium sweet potatoes (7 oz/200 g), peeled and cut into bite-sized pieces

1 portion Cucumber Relish (page 22)

MAKE THE YELLOW CURRY PASTE AND CUCUMBER RELISH by following the recipes on pages 20 and 22.

Place the coconut cream in a heavy-based pot on medium heat and boil until it separates. Add the Curry Paste and fry until fragrant and you can smell the spices.

Add the chicken and continue to fry until the chicken pieces take on color. Add the palm sugar and fish sauce, stirring continuously until the sugar is dissolved. Pour over the coconut milk and bring to a boil, reduce and simmer for 15 minutes.

Add the sweet potato and continue to simmer until it is easily pierced by a skewer. This should allow the chicken enough time to cook through. Leave to rest on the stove with the heat off for 15 minutes to help the flavors develop.

Before serving, check the seasoning: it should taste sweet, salty and aromatic. Serve with the Cucumber Relish.

jungle curry fish with vegetables

THIS CURRY IS ALSO DELICIOUS MADE WITH GROUND DUCK OR RABBIT.

SERVES 4

8 oz (250 g) white fish fillets, skinned
1 clove garlic, peeled
2 green bird's-eye chilies
⅓ cup (100 ml) oil
1 tablespoon chopped Chinese keys (*krachai*)
2 tablespoons Jungle Curry Paste (page 17)
4 kaffir lime leaves
10 pea eggplants (optional)
⅓ cup (100 ml) fish sauce
½ teaspoon superfine (caster) sugar
1 tablespoon oyster sauce
1¼ cups (300 ml) Chicken Stock (page 65) or fish stock

2 apple eggplants or 1 long eggplant, cut into chunks
2 green finger-length chilies, deseeded and cut into lengths
2 yard beans or 12 green beans, cut into lengths
3 baby corns, cut lengthwise
½ cup (20 g) holy basil leaves
¼ cup (12 g) sawtooth herb, very thinly sliced
2 tablespoons Crispy-Fried Shallots (page 23)

MAKE THE JUNGLE CURRY PASTE AND CRISPY-FRIED SHALLOTS by following the recipes on pages 17 and 23.

Hand-chop the fish fillets to a rough paste.

In a mortar and pestle, pound the garlic and chilies to a uniform paste.

Heat the oil in a wok until just smoking. Add the garlic paste and chopped Chinese keys and fry until light brown and it smells nutty. Add the Curry Paste and fry until fragrant and the oil is released from the paste.

Add the lime leaves and pea eggplants (if using). Season with fish sauce, sugar and oyster sauce.

Add the stock and simmer for 1–2 minutes, then add the apple eggplant or long eggplant and chilies. Taste for seasoning—it should be hot and salty at this point, with the sugar just balancing the saltiness.

Add the beans, baby corns and the ground fish. When you put the fish in, stir so that it doesn't clump together. Simmer for 1 minute, then add the basil. Remove from the heat and spoon onto a serving plate.

Garnish with the sawtooth herb and Crispy-Fried Shallots, and serve.

Seafood

smoked fish salad

SERVES 4 AS PART OF A SHARED MEAL

1 portion Smoking Mix (page 20)
1 square piece (8 in/20 cm) banana leaf
1 lb (500 g) white fish fillets
Lime wedges, to serve

Salad
1 medium cucumber, halved and shaved
8 cherry tomatoes, halved
1 green onion (scallion), very finely sliced
1 red finger-length chili, deseeded and very
  finely sliced
½ cup (25 g) coriander leaves (cilantro)

¼ cup (10 g) mint leaves
2 tablespoons roasted peanuts, crushed, plus
  some extra to garnish

Dressing
¾ cup (200 ml) Sweet Vinegar (page 23)
2 tablespoons black Chinese vinegar
1 tablespoon thick sweet soy sauce
⅓ cup (100 ml) lime juice
2–4 green bird's-eye chilies, finely sliced
¼ teaspoon ground red pepper

MAKE THE SMOKING MIX by following the recipe on page 20.

Line a wok with foil. Place the Smoking Mix ingredients on the foil in the wok. Make sure the kitchen is well-ventilated. Turn the heat to high and start to smoke the ingredients.

Line a steamer basket with a banana leaf and place the fish on it. The leaves should be large enough for the fish to sit on, but not cover all the steamer holes. Place the steamer in the smoking wok, turn off the heat and cover with the steamer lid. Let the smoke infuse into the fish for about 5 minutes. This method gives the fish a caramelized, smoky flavor and does not actually cook it.

TO MAKE THE SALAD, toss all the ingredients together in a bowl and set aside.

TO MAKE THE DRESSING, whisk all the ingredients in a bowl. The Dressing should be sharp tasting, with the sharpness being mellowed by the sweet soy and black Chinese vinegar.

TO COOK THE FISH, either steam or pan-sear it. Both methods will take about 5 minutes.

Leave the fish fillet to rest for 2–3 minutes, then break up the fish into the Salad. Add the Dressing, toss and transfer to a serving plate. Place some extra peanuts on top and serve with lime wedges on the side.

salt and pepper fried crab

SERVES 4 AS PART OF A SHARED MEAL

3 lbs (1½ kg) fresh crabs
Splash of fish sauce
²⁄₃ cup (100 g) tapioca flour or a mixture of
   rice flour and cornstarch

Oil, for deep-frying
1 portion Salt and Pepper Mix (page 20)
2 red finger-length chilies, finely sliced
Sweet Soy and Ginger Dressing (page 16)

MAKE THE SWEET SOY AND GINGER DRESSING AND THE SALT AND PEPPER MIX by following the recipes on pages 16 and 20.

If you buy your crabs live, kill it humanely by turning the crab on its back and inserting a knife through the point where the back flaps meet. Leave for 2–3 minutes.

Use your fingers to pull the top shells of the crabs away from their bodies. Discard the gills and innards and rinse the crabs under cold running water. Use a cleaver or sharp knife to cut each crab into quarters (legs and claws attached). Crack the claws with a mallet or the back of a cleaver to help them cook evenly and let the flavors get in.

Toss the crab in the fish sauce, then dust with the tapioca flour or a mixture of rice flour with a bit of cornstarch added.

Heat the oil in a wok until just smoking and add the crab. Cook until the shells turn red and the crab is cooked, about 4 minutes. Remove and drain on paper towels.

Dust the crab with the Salt and Pepper Mix. Garnish with the chilies, and serve with a small bowl of the Dressing.

grilled stuffed calamari

SERVES 4

8 small squids (calamari), about 1 lb (500 g)

Filling
2 cloves garlic, peeled
4 coriander (cilantro) roots, scraped and cleaned
½ teaspoon white peppercorns, ground
1 teaspoon sea salt
4 oz (100 g) black Chinese fungus, soaked in warm water for 30 minutes to reconstitute, then drained and sliced into thin strips
8 water chestnuts, peeled and diced

7 oz (200 g) ground pork
1 teaspoon superfine (caster) sugar
2 teaspoons fish sauce

Salad
½ cup (100 g) Carrot and Daikon Mix (page 22)
10 Vietnamese mint leaves
½ cup (25 g) coriander leaves (cilantro), plus extra to garnish
⅓ cup (15 g) mint leaves
2 tablespoons roasted peanuts, crushed, plus extra to garnish

TO MAKE THE FILLING, first pound the garlic, coriander roots, peppercorns and salt together in a mortar and pestle.

Mix the pounded ingredients, black fungus and water chestnuts into the ground pork with the sugar and fish sauce. Combine all the ingredients together and mix well to expel all the air. Set aside.

Clean the squids by pulling out the tentacles and ink sacs. Reserve the tentacles, discarding the ink and the beaks. Wash out the squid tubes, peel off the skins and discard. Cut off the wings and reserve for another use.

Fill the squid tubes with the Filling, making a small incision at the ends of the tubes to expel any air. Fill to about three-quarters full as the Filling will expand as it cooks. Secure the openings with wooden toothpicks.

Set a steamer over boiling water and steam the squid tubes for 5 minutes until just cooked—this is the best stage to remove them if you are making them in advance. Remove from the steamer.

Heat a barbecue or broiler and place the squid tubes on it to brown the outside and to give some color. Broil or grill the reserved tentacles to serve with the finished dish.

TO MAKE THE SALAD, PREPARE THE CARROT AND DAIKON MIX by following the recipe on page 22, then toss the ingredients together to mix well. Place on a serving platter.

To serve, slice the tubes on a diagonal and place on top of the Salad along with the grilled tentacles. Garnish with extra coriander leaves and peanuts, and serve.

deep-fried whole fish with thai sweet-sour-spicy sauce

OCEAN PERCH, BABY SNAPPER, WHITING OR RIVER TROUT ALL WORK EQUALLY WELL IN THIS DISH.

SERVES 4

1 whole fish, about 1¾ lbs (800 g)
Oil, for deep-frying
½ cup (20 g) holy basil leaves
2 kaffir lime leaves, very finely sliced
1 red finger-length chili, very finely sliced
Lime wedges, to serve

Thai Sweet-Sour-Spicy Sauce
1 coriander (cilantro) root, scraped and
    cleaned
1 in (2½ cm) fresh turmeric root, peeled or 1
    teaspoon ground turmeric
2 red bird's-eye chilies
3 red finger-length chilies, deseeded
3 small shallots, peeled
1 teaspoon dried shrimp paste, roasted
1 tablespoon chopped Chinese keys (*krachai*)
Oil, for frying
1 cup (200 g) shaved palm sugar
3 tablespoons dried tamarind pulp mixed
    with ½ cup hot water, mashed and
    strained to obtain the juice
1 tablespoon sea salt or fish sauce
1 cup (100 g) peeled and diced fresh
    pineapple

TO MAKE THE THAI SWEET-SOUR-SPICY SAUCE, pound the coriander root, turmeric, chilies, shallots, shrimp paste and chopped Chinese keys in a mortar and pestle until a uniform paste is achieved.

Heat a little oil in a pan and fry the paste until crisp and fragrant. Add the palm sugar and a tablespoon of water to help dissolve the sugar. Keep cooking until the sugar caramelizes slightly, then add the tamarind juice, salt and pineapple and simmer for about 5 minutes to allow the pineapple to soften. Keep warm.

Score the fish on both sides. Heat the oil in a wok and deep-fry the fish until crisp. Drain on paper towels, then transfer to a serving plate. Fry the basil leaves in the oil until crisp. Drain.

Pour the sauce over the fish and garnish with the crisp basil, lime leaves and chili. Serve with steamed jasmine rice and fresh lime wedges.

stir-fried crab with chili Jam

DELICIOUS AS AN INDULGENT MEAL FOR TWO. SERVE WITH STEAMED RICE.

SERVES 2

One 2-lb (1-kg) fresh crab in the shell
3 tablespoons oil, for stir-frying
2 red finger-length chilies, deseeded and very
   finely sliced
2 cloves garlic, peeled and crushed
3 kaffir lime leaves
¾ cup (200 ml) Chili Jam (page 14)

⅓ cup (100 ml) Chicken Stock (page 65)
3 tablespoons oyster sauce
3 tablespoons fish sauce
⅓ cup (50 g) superfine (caster) sugar
2 green onions (scallions), cut into thirds
1 cup (40 g) Thai basil leaves

MAKE THE CHILI JAM by following the recipe on page 14.

   For best results, steam the crab first. If you buy your crab live, kill it humanely by turning the crab on its back and inserting a knife through the point where the back flaps meet. Leave for 2–3 minutes.

   Set a steamer set over boiling water and steam the crab for 7 minutes.

   Remove the crab from the steamer. Lift up the flap and remove and discard the spongy gills inside. Cut the crab into 6 pieces. Reserve any liquid from inside the crab and any mustard for adding to the sauce.

   Heat the oil in a wok until just smoking. Add the chilies, garlic and lime leaves. Stir-fry for 30 seconds, then add the Chili Jam, stock, oyster and fish sauces and sugar and reduce the heat. Toss in the crab and any reserved juices and mustard. Toss to coat the crab completely with the sauce, then add the green onions and basil. Mix well to combine the flavors. (If the crab is still a little raw, place a lid on the wok and let it cook over low heat for 2 more minutes.)

   Spoon onto a serving plate and serve with steamed jasmine rice.

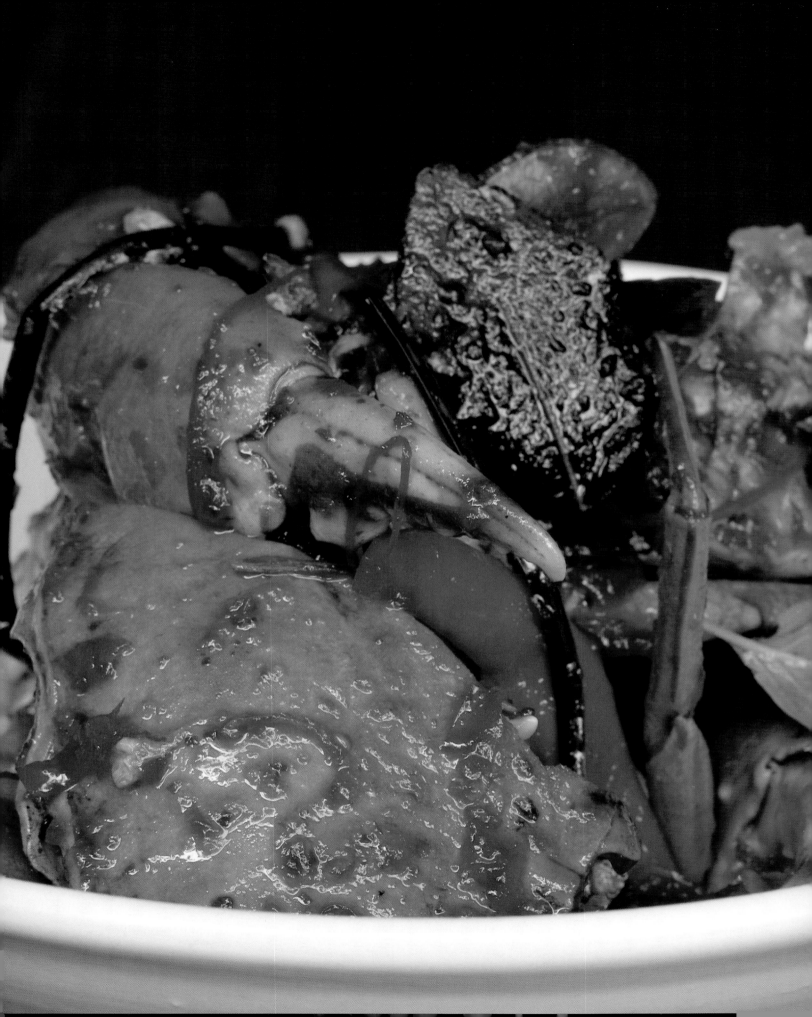

whole roasted baby snapper with sweet soy dressing

SERVES 4 AS PART OF A SHARED MEAL

1 whole baby snapper (about 2 lbs/1 kg), or other whole-fleshed fish, cleaned and scored, or 1¼ lbs (600 g) fish fillets
3 limes
1 bunch coriander leaves (cilantro)

⅔ cup (150 ml) Sweet Soy Dressing (page 15)
2 red finger-length chilies, deseeded and very finely sliced

MAKE THE SWEET SOY DRESSING by following the recipe on page 15.

Preheat the oven to 350°F (180°C).

Place the fish on an oiled baking sheet.

Cut 2 limes in half and place in the cavity of the fish with some coriander stalks. Pour the Sweet Soy Dressing over the fish and place in the oven. Bake for 10 minutes.

Open the oven and baste the fish, then increase the temperature to 400°F (200°C) and bake for a further 5 minutes. The skin should be golden brown and crisp.

Remove the pan from the oven and place the fish on a serving tray. Garnish with the remaining lime, cut into wedges, and chilies. Serve with steamed jasmine rice.

steamed whole fish with sweet soy dressing

SERVES 4 AS PART OF A SHARED MEAL

2 cups (100 g) finely sliced cabbage
2 green onions (scallions), cut into lengths
5 oyster mushrooms
1 in (2½ cm) ginger root, finely sliced
1¾ lbs (800 g) snapper, left whole and scored on both sides, or 1 lb (500 g) fish fillets
⅔ cup (150 ml) Sweet Soy Dressing (page 15)

¾ cup (200 ml) Chicken Stock (page 65) or fish stock
½ cup (25 g) coriander leaves (cilantro), for garnish
½ teaspoon ground white pepper
Finely sliced ginger shreds

MAKE THE SWEET SOY DRESSING by following the recipe on page 15.

Place the cabbage, green onions, mushrooms, ginger and snapper in a deep plate or bowl.

Reserve 1 tablespoon of the Sweet Soy Dressing for garnish and combine the rest with the stock in a saucepan. Bring to a boil and pour over the fish.

Set a steamer large enough to hold the plate over boiling water. Place the bowl with the fish in the steamer and steam for 15 minutes.

Check the fish after 15 minutes. If the flesh comes away easily from the bone the snapper is ready.

Mix the coriander leaves, pepper and ginger with the reserved Sweet Soy Dressing and pour over the fish. Serve with steamed jasmine rice.

deep-fried fish with hot and sour broth

WHEN THE FISH IS COOKED THROUGH, THE FLESH EASILY LIFTS OFF THE BONE. YOU CAN FINISH COOKING THE FISH IN THE HOT SOUP STOCK; AS LONG AS YOU DO NOT BOIL THE SOUP, THE FISH WILL NOT BREAK UP.

SERVES 6 AS PART OF A SHARED MEAL

3 cups (750 ml) Chicken Stock (page 65) or vegetable stock
3 kaffir lime leaves
1 stalk lemongrass, tender inner part of bottom third only, bruised
2–4 red bird's-eye chilies
5 slices galangal root
3 tablespoons fish sauce
1 tablespoon Chili Jam (page 14)
½ tablespoon oyster sauce
4 small shallots, peeled and halved
2 coriander (cilantro) roots, scraped and cleaned

6 oyster mushrooms, cut into bite-sized pieces
1 tomato, cut into bite-sized pieces
Splash of fish sauce
1 whole ocean perch (about 1¾ lbs/800 g) or other white-fleshed fish, cleaned and scaled
Oil, for deep-frying
Juice of 1 lime
1 bunch sawtooth herb, finely shredded
Coriander leaves (cilantro), to garnish

MAKE THE CHILI JAM by following the recipe on page 14.

Bring the stock to a boil in a saucepan and add the lime leaves, lemongrass, chilies, galangal, fish sauce, Chili Jam, oyster sauce, shallots and coriander roots. Reduce the heat and simmer for 2–3 minutes to infuse the flavors. Check the seasoning—it should be hot, sour and salty.

Add the mushrooms and tomato. Simmer for another 3 minutes. Remove from the heat and set aside.

Rub the fish sauce over the fish.

Heat the oil in a wok until just smoking and gently lower the fish into the oil. If the fish is fully immersed, fry until golden brown, 6–7 minutes. If the fish is not fully immersed, be sure to turn the fish so that it cooks evenly. Remove and drain on paper towels.

In a serving bowl, add the lime juice and sawtooth herb.

Put the fish into the bowl and pour over the hot soup. Garnish with coriander leaves and serve with extra Chili Jam on the side.

seared tuna with sweet pork and tangy kaffir lime dressing

7 oz (200 g) fresh tuna fillet
2 portions Green Chili Nahm Jim Sauce (page 14)
Juice of 1 kaffir lime
Crispy-Fried Shallots (page 23)

Salad
½ cup (25 g) coriander leaves (cilantro)
½ cup (20 g) mint leaves
1¼ in (3 cm) ginger root, very finely sliced
1 red finger-length chili, deseeded and very finely sliced

Sweet Pork
2 cloves garlic, peeled
2 coriander (cilantro) roots, scraped and cleaned
1 small ginger root, peeled
1 star anise pod
4 white peppercorns
7 oz (200 g) pork shoulder (pork neck)
¾ cup (200 ml) oil
1 cup (200 g) shaved palm sugar
⅓ cup (100 ml) fish sauce
⅓ cup (100 ml) water

MAKE THE CRISPY-FRIED SHALLOTS by following the recipe on page 23.

TO MAKE THE SWEET PORK, pound the garlic, coriander roots, ginger, star anise and peppercorns in a mortar and pestle until a uniform paste.

Place the pork neck in a steamer set over boiling water and steam until cooked through, about 20 minutes. Remove and cool. Dice the pork into ½ in (1 cm) cubes.

Heat the oil in a wok until just smoking. Fry the pork until golden and crisp. Remove and drain well on paper towels.

Pour off half the oil. Heat the remaining oil and fry the paste until it smells nutty and brown. Add the palm sugar and allow to lightly caramelize. Then add the fish sauce and water. Add the pork to the wok, mix and take off the heat.

Heat a pan or grill and sear the tuna in a little oil until rare. Take off the heat and slice into ½ in (1 cm) strips. Place on a serving plate, and spoon over the Sweet Pork.

MAKE THE GREEN CHILI NAHM JIM SAUCE by following the recipe on page 14, adding the kaffir lime juice for extra flavor.

TO MAKE THE SALAD, combine all the ingredients together, mix well and moisten with the dressing.

Place the Salad on the fish and pork, and garnish with some Crispy-Fried Shallots.

stir-fried shrimp with chili and basil

SERVES 4 AS PART OF A SHARED MEAL

3 tablespoons oil
8 fresh jumbo shrimp, body shell removed
   and deveined, heads and tails left on
2 tablespoons oyster sauce
1 tablespoon superfine (caster) sugar
2 tablespoons fish sauce
²⁄₃ cup (150 ml) Chicken Stock (page 65)
2 green onions (scallions), cut into lengths
1 red finger-length chili, deseeded and cut
   into thin strips
½ cup (20 g) Thai basil leaves

Paste
1 red finger-length chili
2 cloves garlic, peeled
½ in (1 cm) fresh turmeric root, peeled
   or ½ teaspoon ground turmeric
2 coriander (cilantro) roots, scraped and
   cleaned
1 teaspoon sea salt

MAKE THE PASTE, by pounding all the ingredients in a mortar and pestle until a uniform paste.

Heat the oil in a wok or heavy-based skillet. Add the Paste and stir-fry until fragrant.

Add the shrimp, toss with paste for 1 minute, then add the oyster sauce, sugar, fish sauce and stock. Taste for seasoning—it should be hot, salty and sweet. Add the green onion, chili and basil, stir to mix through and spoon onto a serving dish. Serve with steamed jasmine rice.

stir-fried fish with ginger and five spice

SERVES 4 AS PART OF A SHARED MEAL

2 cups (500 ml) oil

1 lb (500 g) white-fleshed fish fillets, cut into bite-sized pieces

⅓ cup (100 ml) fish sauce

⅔ cup (100 g) tapioca flour or a combination of rice flour and cornstarch

2 cloves garlic, minced

2 tablespoons very finely sliced ginger

8 snowpeas

1 red finger-length chili, deseeded and roughly chopped

2 green onions (scallions), cut into lengths

5 garlic chive flowers

2 stalks Chinese celery, cut into lengths

3 tablespoons rice wine or sherry

2 tablespoons oyster sauce

3 tablespoons fish sauce

2 tablespoons superfine (caster) sugar

⅓ cup (100 ml) Chicken Stock (page 65)

Juice of ½ lemon

1 teaspoon Salt and Pepper Mix (page 20)

½ cup (25 g) coriander leaves (cilantro)

Lemon wedges, to serve

MAKE THE SALT AND PEPPER MIX by following the recipe on page 20.

Heat the oil in a wok until just smoking.

Toss the fish in the fish sauce, then dredge in the flour.

Fry the fish until golden brown, then remove from the oil and drain on paper towels. Set aside.

Drain off the excess oil, leaving 3 tablespoons in the wok. Add the garlic and ginger and fry until fragrant. Add the snowpeas, chili, green onions, garlic chives and celery, and stir-fry for 2 minutes, then add the fish.

Deglaze the wok with rice wine or sherry and add the oyster and fish sauces, sugar and stock. Toss through and taste for seasoning—it should be salty and sweet. Add the lemon juice and Salt and Pepper Mix.

Toss through half the coriander leaves and spoon onto a serving plate. Garnish with the rest of the coriander leaves and some extra lemon wedges.

stir-fried squid with a light coconut curry sauce

10 oz (300 g) fresh squid
2 cloves garlic, peeled
2 coriander (cilantro) roots, scraped and
    cleaned
1 in (2½ cm) ginger root, peeled
3 tablespoons oil, for frying
1 small pickling onion, peeled and sliced
2 red finger-length chilies, deseeded and
    chopped
1 tablespoon Homemade Curry Powder (page
    16)

1 tablespoon fish sauce
1 tablespoon oyster sauce
1 teaspoon superfine (caster) sugar
⅓ cup (100 ml)) coconut cream
⅓ cup (100 ml) Chicken Stock (see
    page 65)
1 stalk Chinese celery, finely sliced
2 green onions (scallions), cut into lengths
½ cup (25 g) coriander leaves (cilantro)

MAKE THE HOMEMADE CURRY POWDER by following the recipe on page 16.

Clean the squids by pulling out the tentacles and ink sacs. Reserve the tentacles for another use, discarding the ink and the beaks. Wash out the squid tubes, peel off the skins and discard. Cut off the wings and reserve for another use. Cut the squid tubes in half along their lengths and score the undersides in a cross-hatch pattern. Cut each tube into about 8 equal pieces.

Pound the garlic, coriander roots and ginger in a mortar and pestle to a uniform paste.

Heat the oil in a wok, add the garlic paste and stir-fry over medium heat until fragrant.

Add the squid, pickling onion and chilies and stir-fry for a minute. Add the curry powder and stir-fry until all ingredients are an even yellow color.

Add the fish and oyster sauces, sugar and finally the coconut cream and stock. Taste for seasoning—the mixture should be spicy, salty, sweet and creamy.

Finish off with the Chinese celery and green onions, and fry for a further 30 seconds.

Serve sprinkled with coriander leaves and a dash of coconut cream if desired, and some steamed jasmine rice.

fish grilled in a banana leaf

CHOOSE FILLETS OF EVEN THICKNESS FOR THIS DISH. IT'S IDEAL FOR BARBECUING. THE YOUNGER THE BANANA LEAF, THE BETTER—IT'S MORE PLIABLE AND EASIER TO WORK WITH. OLDER LEAVES CAN BE BRITTLE, AND WILL NEED BLANCHING BEFORE USE.

SERVES 4 AS PART OF A SHARED MEAL

⅓ cup (100 ml) oil

3 tablespoons Rich Red Curry Paste (page 18)

1 tablespoon shaved palm sugar

3 tablespoons fish sauce

1 large piece banana leaf

1 lb (500 g) white-fleshed fish fillets

4 kaffir lime leaves, very finely sliced

2 red finger-length chilies, deseeded and very finely sliced

15 Thai basil leaves

⅓ cup (100 ml) coconut cream

MAKE THE RICH RED CURRY PASTE by following the recipe on page 18.

Heat the oil in a pan to a moderate heat. Add the Curry Paste and fry until the oil releases from the paste. Add the sugar and fish sauce and taste for seasoning. It should be hot, salty and sweet. Let the paste cool for 5 minutes in a mixing bowl.

Meanwhile, scald the banana leaf by pouring boiling water over it in a tub or basin and allow it to sit for 1 minute, then place the banana leaf on a work surface and wipe clean with a damp cloth. Cut out and discard the middle rib.

Smear the paste all over the fish and place on the banana leaf. Sprinkle with the lime leaves, chili, 5 of the basil leaves and half the coconut cream. Bring the middle and ends of the banana leaf together and secure in the middle with a wooden toothpick.

Set a grill or broiler to medium–high heat. Place the banana leaf parcel on the grill, turning every 2 minutes to ensure even cooking. The length of cooking time depends on the thickness of the fish and the heat of your grill. If you do not have a grill, you can cook the parcel on a tray in an oven preheated to 350°F (180°C) for about 15 minutes.

Remove the parcel from the heat. Open the banana leaf and place the fish on a serving plate. Garnish with the remaining basil and drizzle over the coconut cream. Serve.

fish braised in Chinese wine

THE BRAISING LIQUID USED IN THIS RECIPE IS DELICIOUS AS A SOUP BROTH. YOU CAN ALSO USE FISH FILLETS, BUT WHOLE FISH IS MORE TRADITIONAL. DAIKON IS ANOTHER GOOD ADDITION. YOU COULD ADD HALF A BLANCHED PIG'S TROTTER TO THE BRAISING LIQUID IF YOU WANT A RICHER RESULT.

SERVES 4 AS PART OF A SHARED MEAL

2 coriander (cilantro) roots, scraped and cleaned
2 star anise pods
2 cloves garlic, peeled and crushed
1 in (2½ cm) ginger root, peeled
½ teaspoon white peppercorns
½ tablespoon oil
3 tablespoons rice wine or sherry
2 tablespoons rock sugar, pounded to a powder
⅓ cup (100 ml) oyster sauce

4 cups (1 liter) Chicken Stock (page 65) or fish stock
1¼ in (3 cm) stick cassia or cinnamon bark
1 whole white-fleshed fish (2 lbs/1 kg), cleaned and scaled, or 1¼ lbs (600 g) fresh fish fillets
Splash of fish sauce
Coriander leaves (cilantro), to garnish
Ground white pepper
Crispy-Fried Garlic (page 23), to garnish

MAKE THE CRISPY-FRIED GARLIC by following the recipe on page 23.

Preheat the oven to 300°F (150°C).

Pound the coriander roots, 1 star anise, garlic, ginger and peppercorns in a mortar and pestle to a uniform paste. Heat a little oil in a heavy-based pot and fry the paste in as little oil as possible until crisp and fragrant.

Deglaze with the cooking wine, then add the rock sugar, oyster sauce and stock. Bring to a boil and skim. Lower the heat to a simmer and taste—it should be sweet, aromatic and salty. Add the cassia or cinnamon bark and remaining star anise. Set aside.

Score the fish on both sides and douse with fish sauce. Drain and place in a braising pan, deep enough to hold all the hot liquid. Cover the fish with the liquid, then cover with baking paper and foil and place in the oven for 20 minutes. After 20 minutes, remove from the oven and discard the foil and baking paper. Let the fish rest for 10 minutes.

To serve, lift the fish out with 2 spatulas and place on a serving dish. It should be fragrant and a light tan color.

Bring the braising liquid back to a simmer, check the seasoning and strain enough liquid over the fish to half cover it. Garnish with coriander leaves, a little white pepper and garlic.

In the remaining liquid, blanch some Chinese broccoli and snowpeas or pea sprouts and serve as a side dish. Sprinkle generously with extra Crispy-Fried Garlic and fresh coriander leaves.

grilled sardines with sweet thai dressing

SERVES 4 AS PART OF A SHARED MEAL

6 whole fresh sardines
Splash of fish sauce
3 tablespoons oil
Crispy-Fried Garlic (page 23)
Crispy-Fried Shallots (page 23)

4 deep-fried red finger-length chilies,
 deseeded
4 tablespoons Sweet Thai Dressing (page 46)
Coriander leaves (cilantro), to garnish
Lime wedges, to serve

MAKE THE CRISPY-FRIED GARLIC AND SHALLOTS by following the recipes on page 23.

To debone the sardines, cut along the underside of the fish. Remove the guts. Wash and place the fish back on the board, belly side up. Gently press down on the fish with your thumb along its length and backbone to flatten. The backbone should now be easily pulled out by breaking the bone closest to the head—and gently pulling out the backbone and ribcage. Flatten the fish so that it is butterflied, with head and tail still intact. Repeat with the remaining fish.

Place all the fish in a bowl and toss with a splash of fish sauce.

Set a grill to medium–high heat, lightly oil and place the fish, skin side down, on the grill and cook until golden brown color. Carefully flip over with a spatula to seal the other side. Sardines cook quickly, so keep an eye on them and don't allow them to overcook.

MAKE THE SWEET THAI DRESSING by following the recipe on page 46.

Place the fish on a serving plate, sprinkle generously with the Crispy-Fried Garlic and Shallots. Break the roasted chilies over the top, drizzle with Sweet Thai Dressing and garnish with coriander leaves. Serve with lime wedges on the side.

grilled tuna with herb salad and thai relish

1½ lbs (700 g) fresh tuna fillets

Thai Relish
8 cloves garlic, peeled
8 small shallots, peeled
2–4 red finger-length chilies, deseeded
1 ripe tomato
1 red bell pepper, roasted and peeled
2 tablespoons shaved palm sugar
3 tablespoons fish sauce
3 tablespoons dried tamarind pulp mixed
    with ½ cup (125 ml) hot water, mashed
    and strained to obtain the jucie

Herb Salad
½ cup (25 g) coriander leaves (cilantro)
¼ cup (10 g) mint leaves
½ stalk lemongrass, tender inner part of
    bottom third only, finely sliced
1½ cups (100 g) finely sliced cabbage
¼ medium cucumber, cut into batons
1 small shallot, peeled and sliced
1 red finger-length chili, deseeded and very
    finely sliced

TO MAKE THE THAI RELISH, dry-roast the garlic, shallots, chilies and tomato in a wok over medium–high heat until soft and caramelized. Put a lid over the wok to finish the cooking and to allow the ingredients to steam.

Remove the ingredients from the wok. Mix with the bell pepper and pound to a rough paste in a mortar and pestle. You may have to do this in batches, depending on the size of your mortar. Stir in the palm sugar, fish sauce and tamarind juice.

Heat a grill to medium–high. Grill the tuna for about 2 minutes on each side, depending on the thickness of the fish, until rare. If you don't have a grill, you can also fry the fish in a pan using a little bit of oil.

Remove from the heat. Break up the fish and place in a serving dish.

TO MAKE THE HERB SALAD, toss all the ingredients together, adding just enough Thai Relish to bind them together.

Place the Salad on the fish and serve with the extra Thai Relish on the side—it is great mixed through hot steamed rice.

salt and pepper calamari with sweet soy and ginger dressing

SERVES 4

8 cups (2 liters) oil, for deep-frying
1 lb (500 g) cleaned fresh cuttlefish or squid
1⅓ cups (200 g) tapioca flour, for dusting
2 portions Salt and Pepper Mix (page 20)
Lemon or lime wedges, to serve
Sweet Soy and Ginger Dressing (page 16)
Coriander leaves (cilantro), to garnish

Batter
1⅔ cups (200 g) rice flour
1⅔ cups (200 g) glutinous rice flour
1⅔ cups (200 g) tapioca flour
1⅔ cups (400 ml) soda water

MAKE THE SWEET SOY AND GINGER DRESSING AND THE SALT AND PEPPER MIX by following the recipes on page 16 and 20.

TO MAKE THE BATTER, sift all the flours into a bowl, then slowly whisk in the soda water to make a thick creamy consistency like pouring cream. Add more soda water if the batter is too thick.

Heat the oil in a wok or a suitably large pan until just smoking.

Score the underside of the squid in a cross-hatch pattern, then cut into ⅛ in (5 mm) strips. Dredge the squid into the flour, then into the batter.

Holding onto one end of the squid, dip half of it into the hot oil for 10 seconds. Then let it fall into the oil. This way, the squid will not stick to the bottom of the pan and instead will float immediately back to the surface. Fry until the batter turns a light golden color, 4–5 minutes, then remove and drain on paper towels.

Continue until all the squid are done. Dust with the Salt and Pepper Mix.

Place on a serving plate with lemon or lime wedges and a small bowl of the Sweet Soy and Ginger Dressing. Garnish with coriander leaves.

Meat

braised beef ribs with sweet thai dressing

SHIN BEEF ALSO WORKS WELL IN PLACE OF THE BEEF RIBS.

SERVES 4 AS PART OF A SHARED MEAL

4 cups (1 liter) oil, for shallow-frying
2 lbs (1 kg) good quality beef ribs
2 cups (500 ml) coconut cream
2 cups (500 ml) Chicken Stock (page 65)
1½ in (4 cm) galangal root, peeled
 and chopped
⅓ cup (100 ml) oyster sauce
4 kaffir lime leaves
1 stalk lemongrass, tender inner part of
 bottom third only,

⅓ cup (100 ml) fish sauce
½ cup (100 g) shaved palm sugar
⅓ cup (100 ml) Sweet Thai Dressing
 (page 46)
1 small shallot, peeled and sliced
Coriander leaves (cilantro), to garnish
Mint leaves, to garnish
Sawtooth herb, very finely sliced, to garnish
Nahm Pla Prik Dipping Sauce (page 16)

MAKE THE NAHM PLA PRIK DIPPING SAUCE AND SWEET THAI DRESSING by following the recipes on pages 16 and 46.

Preheat the oven to 350°F (180°C).

Heat the oil in a wok and shallow-fry the ribs until brown and caramelized. Drain well and place in a deep braising pan.

In a heavy-based pot, combine the coconut cream, stock, galangal, oyster sauce, lime leaves and lemongrass and bring to a boil. Season with the fish sauce and palm sugar.

We're looking for a tasty base—after using it for braising, the liquid can be reduced for use as a sauce or as a base for a curry. Pour the braising liquid over the beef, cover with a lid or baking paper and foil and braise for 1½–2 hours. Remove the pan from the oven and let the ribs cool in the liquid.

Remove the ribs from the stock. Strain and reserve the liquid. You could also season it, and shred the beef back into the liquid and serve as a soup.

Set a broiler to medium–high heat. Broil the ribs until caramelized on the outside. Place the ribs on a serving plate and drizzle with the Sweet Thai Dressing and garnish with the shallots, coriander leaves, mint and sawtooth herb. Serve with the Nahm Pla Prik Dipping Sauce.

barbecued pork

Use this pork in stir-fries and salads, or just enjoy on its own with jasmine rice, soy sauce and chili. It's worth having in the fridge for snacks, so the quantities given here are generous.

SERVES 6 AS PART OF A SHARED MEAL

4 tablespoons fermented bean curd
3 tablespoons light soy sauce
5 tablespoons rice wine or sherry
4 tablespoons hoisin sauce
3 tablespoons yellow bean paste

4 tablespoons superfine (caster) sugar
4 cloves garlic, peeled
4 lbs (2 kg) pork shoulder (pork neck) quartered

Mix all the ingredients except the pork together and blend to a smooth paste.

Marinate the pork in the paste for as little as 2 hours or overnight—the longer the better.

When you're ready to cook, preheat the oven to 350°F (180°C).

Place the pork sections on a rack over a large baking pan, and half-fill the pan with water. This will help to stop the meat from drying out during cooking.

Roast the pork for 35–40 minutes or until golden and fragrant. Rest the meat for 10–15 minutes. Slice finely and serve with steamed jasmine rice and some Chinese greens.

pork, crab & beansprout omelet

Serves 4

⅓ cup (100 ml) oil
4 eggs, beaten
¾ cup (150 g) cooked ground pork
2½ cups (150 g) cooked crabmeat
½ teaspoon ground white pepper
1 teaspoon sea salt

1 in (2½ cm) ginger root, peeled
  and very finely sliced
1 green onion (scallion), cut into
  fine rounds
1 cup (50 g) fresh beansprouts

Heat the oil in a wok or non-stick pan until just smoking and add the beaten eggs. The mixture will bubble around the edges (if you are using a well-seasoned wok, it will not stick).

Gently move the egg with a spatula to help the egg cook. Add the rest of the ingredients to the middle of the egg. When you have done this, push gently down with the spatula; the egg will ooze out towards the edges. Let the egg brown for 30 seconds, then turn out onto a large serving plate.

This is great served with Cucumber Relish (page 22).

caramelized pork hock
with chili vinegar dip

FOR A COMPLETE DISH TO HAVE WITH RICE, STEAM SOME CHINESE BROCCOLI AND PLACE IT UNDERNEATH THE PORK HOCKS.

SERVES 6–8

Oil for deep-frying
2 pork hocks (picnic shoulder) with bone-in
  (about 2 kgs/1 lb)
1 quantity Master Stock (page 65)
Crispy-Fried Shallots (page 23)
Coriander leaves (cilantro), to garnish
1 red finger-length chili, very finely sliced

½ portion Chili Vinegar Dipping Sauce
  (page 15)

Caramel Sauce
2½ cups (500 g) shaved palm sugar
1 stick cassia or cinnamon bark
1 star anise pod

MAKE THE MASTER STOCK by following the recipe on page 65.

MAKE THE CRISPY-FRIED SHALLOTS AND CHILI VINEGAR DIPPING SAUCE by following the recipes on pages 23 and 15.

Heat the oil in a wok until just smoking and deep-fry the pork hocks, one at a time, until golden brown, 4–5 minutes. Remove from the oil and drain well on paper towels.

Bring the Master Stock to a boil in a large heavy-based pan. Add the pork hocks and simmer for 1½–2 hours over medium heat. To test for readiness, the pork hocks should be quite soft to the touch. Remove the hocks from the stock and cool. Reserve 1 cup (250 ml) of the braising liquid for the Sauce.

When cool, grab the hock bone and twist—the whole bone should come out, leaving only the meat. Push the hock together to form a dense mass and refrigerate until set and firm, 3–4 hours.

TO MAKE THE CARAMEL SAUCE, place the palm sugar in a heavy-based pot and add a splash of water to help it melt. Allow the sugar to caramelize, then stop the cooking by adding the reserved braising liquid, cassia or cinnamon bark and star anise to give it a good flavor. The Caramel Sauce should be quite savory and not too runny—a honey-like consistency. If too runny, keep reducing the stock until a sauce consistency. Check the seasoning: if it's too sweet, add ⅓ cup (100 ml) of fish sauce to cut the sweetness.

To serve, cut the pork hocks into bite-sized pieces.

Reheat the oil used for deep-frying the hocks in a wok and deep-fry the meat until crisp and golden, 5–6 minutes. Drain on paper towels.

To serve, place in a bowl and pour the warm Caramel Sauce over the meat. Garnish with some Crispy-Fried Shallots, coriander leaves and chili. Serve with the Chili Vinegar Dipping Sauce on the side.

stir-fried beef with black bean sauce

SERVES 4 AS PART OF A SHARED MEAL

3 tablespoons oil

1 tablespoon grated ginger root

2 cloves garlic, peeled and minced

10 oz (300 g) beef chunk or sirloin, finely sliced

3 tablespoons rice wine or sherry

1 tablespoon Black Bean Sauce (page 16)

⅓ cup (100 ml) Chicken Stock (page 65)

1 tablespoon superfine (caster) sugar

1 piece pickled mustard cabbage (*kiam chye*), sliced

10 snowpeas

2 red finger-length chilies, deseeded and chopped

Coriander leaves (cilantro), to garnish

MAKE THE BLACK BEAN SAUCE by following the recipe on page 16.

Heat the oil in a wok until just smoking and fry the ginger and garlic until nutty and fragrant. Add the beef and stir-fry until it changes color. Deglaze with the rice wine or sherry and add the Black Bean Sauce.

Add the Chicken Stock and sugar, then add the pickled mustard cabbage, snowpeas and chili. Stir-fry for 2 minutes until all the ingredients are well coated and cooked through.

Taste for seasoning—it should be salty and sweet. There should be some liquid for sauce; if too dry, add a little more Chicken Stock or water. Taste for seasoning, adjusting as necessary.

Remove from the heat and transfer to a serving plate. Garnish with coriander leaves.

homemade pork & peanut sausages

You can purchase sausage casings from your butcher. If you are making these sausages in advance, omit the basil leaves, as they tend to blacken if left for more than a few hours before cooking.

Serves 4 as part of a shared meal

1½ cups (300 g) lean ground pork
1½ cups (300 g ground pork fatback
½ cup (100 g) Peanut Curry Paste (page 18)
5 kaffir lime leaves, very thinly sliced
2 tablespoons sea salt
¾ cup (150 g) shaved palm sugar

⅔ cup (100 g) roasted peanuts, crushed
1 cup (40 g) Thai basil leaves, roughly chopped
3 ft (1 meter) pigs' intestines, cleaned and
   rinsed thoroughly
Oil
Banana leaf

Make the Peanut Curry Paste by following the recipe on page 18.

Combine both types of ground pork in a large mixing bowl. Add the Curry Paste, lime leaves and salt and mix well together. Add the palm sugar, then the peanuts and basil. Mix well together and pick up small handfuls of the mixture and throw it back into the mixing bowl. Repeat this process for about 5 minutes so that all possible air is expelled. Before you pipe the mixture, fry a little of the filling in oil and taste to check the seasoning.

Wash the intestines well. Push one end over the spout of a tap and slowly run some cold water through it to check for holes.

Spoon the pork mixture into a piping bag with a nozzle attached, then place the intestine over the nozzle. When the entire intestine has been fed on, tie a knot at one end of the intestine and start piping the mix, sliding the intestine off the nozzle as it fills with the mixture. Coil the sausage into a spiral and place on a stainless or plastic tray as you go along. There should be enough mixture to make a sausage to fill a small steamer, about 8 in (20 cm) across. Brush the sausage with some oil so it won't dry out.

Set a steamer over boiling water and place the sausage on a piece of banana leaf. Poke a few holes in it with a skewer so the sausages won't split when cooking. Steam for 10 minutes, then remove the sausage and let it cool slightly.

You can prepare the sausage in advance until this stage. To keep, brush with some oil and refrigerate.

To cook the sausage, place under a preheated broiler or on a grill and cook the sausage until the skin is caramelized and smells fragrant, 4–6 minutes. Remove from the heat and rest for 5–10 minutes.

To serve, cut the sausage at an angle. The sausages are great on their own or served on a betel leaf with some fresh chili and finely sliced ginger. Or make a salad with some ginger, coriander leaves and small shallots, tossed with a simple dressing of Sweet Chili Sauce (page 15) and lime juice.

grilled pork with fennel seeds

THE PORK FROM THIS RECIPE CAN ALSO BE COOKED INTO A GREEN CURRY.

Serves 4

2 tablespoons fennel seeds

1 tablespoon sea salt

1 lb (500 g) pork shoulder (pork neck)

4 tablespoons thick sweet soy sauce

Pound the fennel and salt to a fine powder in a mortar and pestle. Rub into the pork and let it sit for 1 hour in the refrigerator.

Set a broiler or grill at medium–high heat.

Rub the thick sweet soy sauce into the meat, then broil on all sides for 8–10 minutes until well caramelized and fragrant, taking care not to burn the outside or the burnt spice will turn bitter.

Rest for 10 minutes before slicing and serving.

soy-braised suckling pig

YOU'LL HAVE TO PRE-ORDER THE SUCKLING PIG FROM A BUTCHER. FLAVOR THE MASTER STOCK WITH LOTS OF AROMATICS SO THAT THE PORK SKIN TAKES ON LOTS OF FLAVOR.

SERVES 4

1¾ lbs (800 g) suckling pig leg
1 portion Master Stock (page 65)
Oil for deep-frying

8–10 star anise pods
2 sticks cassia or cinnamon bark
½ cup sliced ginger root

MAKE THE MASTER STOCK by following the recipe on page 65.

Put the pork leg, Master Stock, spices and ginger in a pan large enough to hold them all, and braise over medium heat for 25–30 minutes. Allow the leg to cool in the stock.

When cool, remove from the stock and allow the pork leg to dry thoroughly. For the best crisp results, place the pork leg in front of a fan set on low or in a well-ventilated area of the kitchen. If you refrigerate, take out of the refrigerator 1–2 hours before frying so that it warms through to the middle and the skin doesn't burn.

Heat the oil in a wok until just smoking. Deep-fry the pork until the skin is a deep golden color and crisp, 5–8 minutes. Remove and drain on paper towels.

Slice and serve with Roasted Eggplant and Chili Relish (page 21) or Sweet Soy Dressing (page 15) and rice.

braised beef shin with thai herbs

The richness of the meaty braising liquid will be balanced by the hot and sour dressing in the salad, giving a good balance of flavors.

Serves 4 as part of a shared meal

Braised Beef
1 lb (500 g) beef shin
2 tablespoons thick sweet soy sauce
⅓ cup (100 ml) oil
5 cloves garlic, peeled
1½ in (4 cm) ginger root, peeled
2 coriander (cilantro) roots, scraped and
  cleaned
1 small red onion
⅓ cup (100 ml) rice wine or sherry
3½ tablespoons (50 g) rock sugar, crushed
⅓ cup (100 ml) oyster sauce
3 cups (750 ml) Chicken Stock (page 65)
3 tablespoons black Chinese vinegar
1 teaspoon sea salt

Herb Salad
3 tablespoons fresh lime juice
½ teaspoon ground red pepper
1 tablespoon fish sauce
2 green bird's-eye chilies, finely sliced
10 coriander leaves (cilantro)
10 mint leaves
1 green onion (scallion), finely shredded
1 small shallot, peeled and finely sliced
½ red finger-length chili, deseeded and finely
  sliced

To make the Braised Beef, rub the thick sweet soy sauce all over the beef. Heat a little oil in a pan and seal the beef on all sides. Place in a deep braising dish.

Pound the garlic, ginger, coriander root and onion to a paste. Heat some oil in a heavy-based saucepan and fry the pounded ingredients until golden brown. Discard the excess oil and deglaze with the rice wine or sherry. Add the rock sugar, oyster sauce and Chicken Stock. Bring to a boil and skim off all the foam. Pour the liquid over the beef. Cover with greaseproof paper and foil, and braise on the stove over low heat for 1½ hours until the meat is soft.

Remove the meat and set aside. Strain the liquid and boil hard to reduce by a third. Add the vinegar and salt and taste—the mixture should taste rich and meaty.

To make the Herb Salad, combine the lime juice, ground red pepper, fish sauce and chilies. This dressing should taste very hot and sour.

In a stainless steel bowl, toss together the rest of the ingredients and add the dressing.

To serve, cut the Braised Beef into ½ in (1 cm) slices and reheat in the reduced braising liquid. Place the sliced beef in the middle of the serving bowl, and pour over a generous amount of the braising liquid.

Place the Herb Salad on top of the beef, and pour some of the dressing into the meaty juices. Serve with steamed rice.

Poultry

stir-fried soy duck with basil

BUY A READY-PREPARED SOY DUCK FROM A CHINESE TAKEAWAY FOR THIS DISH OR PREPARE YOUR OWN BY FOLLOWING THE RECIPE ON PAGE 135. IF YOU ARE BUYING THE DUCK, ASK FOR A CONTAINER OF DUCK JUICES AS WELL. IF YOU'VE COOKED THE DUCK AT HOME, YOU CAN USE THE MASTER STOCK IN PLACE OF THE CHICKEN STOCK.

SERVES 4 AS PART OF A SHARED MEAL

1 whole Soy Duck (page 135)
3 tablespoons oil
2 red finger-length chilies, deseeded and cut into bite-sized pieces
2 cloves garlic, peeled and pounded
1½ in (4 cm) ginger root, peeled and very finely sliced
⅓ cup (100 ml) rice wine or sherry
1 green onion (scallion), cut into lengths

4 wingbeans or 12 green beans, cut into lengths
⅓ cup (100 ml) duck juices or Chicken Stock (page 65)
3 tablespoons oyster sauce
⅓ cup (50 g) superfine (caster) sugar
3 tablespoons fish sauce
3 tablespoons soy sauce
½ cup (20 g) Thai basil leaves

Cut the duck down the middle and remove the rib bones. Cut the leg in half and the breast into quarters. You can get the restaurant to chop it for you in this way.

Heat the oil in a wok or pan and add the chilies, garlic and ginger. Stir-fry until fragrant for 20 seconds, taking care not to burn the garlic or it will turn bitter.

Deglaze the wok with rice wine or sherry, add the duck, green onion and beans. Then add the duck juices or stock, oyster sauce, sugar, fish and soy sauces. Taste—it should be rich and full flavored. Add the basil leaves to finish. Serve with steamed rice.

duck with red curry

Use the braised duck from the recipe for Braised Duck Salad with Cashews, Beansprouts & Hoisin Dressing (page 139) for this dish.

Serves 4 as part of a shared meal

4 cooked duck legs (marylands)
1 clove garlic, peeled and crushed
1 red bird's-eye chili
1½ cups (375 ml) oil, for shallow-frying
½ cup (20 g) holy basil leaves
2 tablespoons chopped Chinese keys (*krachai*)
2 tablespoons Light Red Curry Paste (page 19)
4 kaffir lime leaves

12 pea eggplants (optional)
2 apple eggplants or 1 long eggplant, cut into chunks
2 red finger-length chilies, deseeded and cut into strips
⅓ cup (100 ml) Chicken Stock (page 65)
2 tablespoons oyster sauce
2 tablespoons fish sauce
1 tablespoon superfine (caster) sugar
1 salted duck egg, boiled and peeled

Make the Light Red Curry Paste by following the recipe on page 19.

Cook the duck legs by following the instructions on page 139. When cooked, cut each leg into 2 pieces, separating the thigh and drumstick.

Pound the garlic and chili in a mortar and pestle to a uniform paste.

Heat the oil in a wok and fry the duck until golden brown on the outside, about 1½ minutes. Remove from the oil and drain on paper towels. Fry the basil leaves in the oil for 1 minute until dark green and crispy but not burnt. Drain and set aside.

Remove the oil from the wok, leaving ⅓ cup (100 ml). Lower the heat to medium, add the garlic and chili paste and ginger and fry until fragrant. Add the curry paste and lime leaves, and cook until the paste is fragrant and no rawness can be detected.

Add the eggplant and chilies and return the duck to the pan. Season with the Chicken Stock, oyster and fish sauces and sugar, and mix well to combine the flavors. At this point, taste—it should be hot, rich and full flavored. If the mixture is too dry, add a little more stock.

Break up the egg and toss with the duck. Spoon onto a serving plate and garnish with the fried basil leaves.

soy duck or chicken

This duck or chicken can be used in all of the recipes that call for duck or chicken bought from a Chinese foodstore. It's also good shredded into the Green Shallot Pancakes (page 22).

Serves 8

1 portion Master Stock (page 65)
1 fresh duck or chicken
Fresh ginger

1 stick cassia or cinnamon bark
1 star anise pod
1 pig's trotter

MAKE THE MASTER STOCK by following the recipe on page 65.

Bring the Master Stock to a boil. If reusing the stock, refresh with extra ginger and spices. (It is good to add extra ginger anyway when cooking chicken.) Add the pig's trotter to the stock.

Wash and pat dry the duck or chicken, removing any excess fat and the tail (parson's nose), especially from the duck as there is a gland within that can make the stock bitter.

Chicken will take 45–50 minutes, and the duck will take about 70 minutes to cook over a gentle simmer. Ducks tend to float, too, so you may need to fit a lid that is slightly smaller than the pot over it to stop the duck from bobbing up.

When done, remove the duck or chicken from the stock and place on a rack to cool.

Before cooking further, for example deep-frying, place the chicken in the refrigerator to cool for the best crisp-skinned results, as the dry, cool air of the fridge will dry out the skin well. Alternatively, place the cooked chicken in front of a fan or use a hair-dryer to dry out the skin.

If cooking further, cut the chicken or duck in half and fry, half at a time, to warm the meat all the way through.

spiced chicken with plum sauce

USE FREE-RANGE CHICKENS IF POSSIBLE AS THEY YIELD MUCH BETTER RESULTS.

SERVES 8 AS PART OF A SHARED MEAL

4 star anise pods
2 sticks cassia or cinnamon bark
1 cup Sichuan peppercorns
4 small dried red chilies
½ cup (140 g) sea salt
1 free-range chicken (about 3 lbs/1½ kgs)
Oil, for deep-frying
1 portion Salt and Pepper Mix (page 20)
Lemon wedges, to serve

Plum Sauce
2½ cups (500 g) shaved palm sugar
⅓ cup (100 ml) water
⅓ cup (100 ml)) fish sauce
3 tablespoons dried tamarind pulp mixed
    with ½ cup (125 ml) hot water, mashed
    and strained to obtain the juice
10 blood plums
⅓ cup (100 ml) hoisin sauce

MAKE THE SALT AND PEPPER MIX by following the recipe on page 20.

Dry-roast the star anise, cassia or cinnamon bark, Sichuan peppercorns and chilies in a heavy-based pan until fragrant. Mix with the salt and grind to a fine powder in a spice grinder or blender.

Dry the chicken with a kitchen towel, and coat thoroughly with the ground spices.

Set a steamer large enough to hold the chicken over boiling water. Place the chicken in the steamer and steam, covered, for 50 minutes on a gentle simmer. When done, remove the

chicken and allow to cool to room temperature. You'll notice the spice coating dry and harden around the chicken, which is essential before it is fried. This can be done in advance.

Heat the oil in a large wok. Cut the chicken in half and fry in the hot oil until the skin is crisp. Drain on paper towels.

TO MAKE THE PLUM SAUCE, melt the sugar in a heavy-based pot with the water. Let the sugar caramelize slightly, then add the fish sauce and tamarind juice. Add the plums and hoisin sauce, and cook until they release their juices. Keep cooking until you get a honey-like consistency again. The mixture should taste sweet, slightly sour and salty. Pass the sauce through a wire mesh strainer to make a rich, red sauce. When reheating, add a few slices of fresh plum to the sauce if desired.

To serve, cut the chicken into 6 pieces and place on a serving platter. Spoon over the sauce. Serve the Salt and Pepper Mix on the side. Garnish with lemon wedges.

soy chicken stir-fried with lotus root and snowpeas

LOTUS ROOT IS GREAT FOR ABSORBING ALL THE FLAVORS FROM THE STIR-FRY. YOU CAN FIND FRESH LOTUS ROOT IN SOME ASIAN GROCERS. FROZEN LOTUS ROOT IS ALSO AVAILABLE BUT IF YOU CANNOT FIND IT, THEN USE SLICED WATER CHESTNUTS INSTEAD. IF YOU'VE POACHED YOUR OWN CHICKEN AT HOME, USE SOME OF THE MASTER STOCK IN PLACE OF THE CHICKEN STOCK.

SERVES 4

3 tablespoons oil
2 red finger-length chilies, deseeded and cut into strips
2 cloves garlic, peeled and crushed
2 tablespoons minced ginger
Splash of rice wine or sherry
½ Soy Chicken (page 135), chopped into chunks

8 snowpeas
8 pieces thinly sliced lotus root
6 oyster mushrooms
⅓ cup (100 ml) Chicken Stock (page 65)
2 tablespoons oyster sauce
2 tablespoons fish sauce
2 tablespoons light soy sauce
2 tablespoons superfine (caster) sugar
2 green onions (scallions), cut into lengths

MAKE THE SOY CHICKEN by following the recipe on page 135.

Heat the oil in a wok until just smoking. Add the chilies, garlic and ginger and fry until fragrant, about 30 seconds. Deglaze with the rice wine or sherry and add the chicken, snowpeas, lotus root and mushrooms. Toss for about 30 seconds, then add the stock, oyster and fish sauces, light soy sauce and sugar. Add the green onions and toss for a further 30 seconds. Taste for seasoning—it should be rich and full flavored.

Spoon onto a serving plate and serve with steamed jasmine rice.

braised duck salad with cashews and hoisin dressing

1 portion Master Stock (page 65)

4 duck legs (marylands), trimmed of excess fat

⅓ cup (100 ml) thick sweet soy sauce

2 cups (500 ml) oil, for shallow-frying

2 tablespoons black Chinese vinegar

1 drop sesame oil

1 tablespoon hoisin sauce

Salad

2 cups (100 g) beansprouts

½ cup (25 g) coriander leaves (cilantro)

6-oz (185-g) can water chestnuts, drained and diced

2 green onions (scallions), very finely sliced

3 tablespoons roasted cashew nuts, lightly crushed

1 red finger-length chili, deseeded and very finely sliced

1¼ in (3 cm) ginger root, peeled and very finely sliced

MAKE THE MASTER STOCK by following the recipe on page 65.

Bring the Master Stock to a boil. If reusing from another recipe, add some extra ginger, star anise and salt to refresh the stock.

Rub the duck legs with the sweet soy. Heat the oil in a wok and shallow-fry the legs until golden brown, about 2 minutes. Transfer the legs to a braising pan and cover with the boiling stock. Braise for 50 minutes on a gentle simmer or until the duck is tender and a rich, deep-brown color. Remove the duck from the braising liquid and cool. Reserve ½ cup (125 ml) of the stock and cool. Taste for seasoning to see how strong it is. If it's too strong in flavor, dilute with a little Chicken Stock or water.

TO MAKE THE SALAD, combine all the ingredients together in a large bowl.

Take the duck meat off the bone and shred. Toss the meat with the Salad, then place on a serving plate.

Add the vinegar, sesame oil and hoisin sauce to the reserved braising liquid to make a dressing and pour over the Salad. Serve with steamed jasmine rice.

stir-fried chicken with basil

THIS RECIPE IS ALSO DELICIOUS MADE WITH SLICED BEEF AND BAMBOO SHOOTS.

SERVES 4 AS PART OF A SHARED MEAL

3 tablespoons oil

7 oz (200 g) boneless chicken breast or thigh, sliced

2 red finger-length chilies, deseeded and cut into strips

1 clove garlic, crushed

2 tablespoons chopped Chinese keys (*krachai*)

1/3 cup (100 ml) Chicken Stock (page 65)

2 tablespoons oyster sauce

2 tablespoons fish sauce

1 tablespoon superfine (caster) sugar

3 yard beans or 18 green beans, cut into lengths

1/2 cup (20 g) holy basil leaves

1 red finger-length chili, very finely sliced

1 kaffir lime leaf, very finely sliced

Heat the oil in a wok until just smoking.

Add the chicken and stir-fry until well colored. Pour off the excess oil, then toss in the chilies, garlic and chopped Chinese keys. Stir-fry for 30 seconds, then add the stock, oyster and fish sauces, sugar and beans. Taste for seasoning—it should be rich and full-flavored. Add the basil, which will give a peppery finish to the dish. Toss to combine the flavors, then spoon onto a serving plate. Garnish with some very finely sliced chili and kaffir lime leaf.

grilled chicken with coconut and basil sauce

SERVES 4

1 spring chicken (about 1 lb/500 g)

1 cup (250 ml) coconut cream

2 stalks lemongrass, tender inner part of bottom third only, bruised

1 teaspoon dried tamarind pulp mixed with 1 tablespoon hot water, mashed and strained to obtain the juice

1 teaspoon shaved palm sugar

2 slices galangal root

Flesh of ½ coconut, grated

2 red finger-length chilies, deseeded and very finely sliced

½ cup (20 g) Thai basil leaves

Spice Paste

3 red finger-length chilies

½ teaspoon dried shrimp paste, roasted in foil

2 cloves garlic, peeled

3 small shallots, peeled

4 slices galangal root

Cut the chicken in half and remove any fatty bits.

TO MAKE THE SPICE PASTE, pound all the ingredients to a uniform paste in a mortar and pestle. Rub the paste into the chicken.

Place the coconut cream, lemongrass, tamarind juice, sugar and galangal in a heavy-based pot large enough to hold the chicken halves. Add the chicken and remaining Spice Paste and simmer gently with the lid off.

Baste the chicken constantly during cooking if not totally submerged, until the chicken is tender, about 20 minutes. Remove from the pot and allow to cool or refrigerate. Reserve the braising liquid.

Heat a chargrill or broiler and roast the chicken over very low heat until the outside is golden and caramelized, about 8 minutes on each side. Remove and place on a serving plate.

Add the coconut, chilies and basil to the reserved braising liquid and taste for seasoning, adjusting if necessary. Pour the mixture over the grilled chicken and serve.

Desserts

durian banana coconut pancakes with palm sugar caramel

DURIANS ARE A TROPICAL FRUIT KNOWN FOR THEIR STRONG SMELL AND SWEET CUSTARDY TEXTURE. THEY ARE AVAILABLE FRESH OR FROZEN FROM ASIAN GROCERS. IF UNAVAILABLE, REPLACE WITH ONE MORE BANANA.

MAKES 12

1½ cups (50 g) grated coconut (if using desiccated coconut, use ½ the amount and reconstitute with warm water)
1 cup (125 g) rice flour
⅓ cup (50 g) tapioca flour
1 tablespoon arrowroot flour or cornstarch
2 ripe bananas, mashed

3 tablespoons (50 g) durian flesh
1 cup (200 g) shaved palm sugar
1 egg
1 cup (250 ml) coconut cream
Oil, for pan frying
6 tablespoons Palm Sugar Caramel (page 23)
Passionfruit Ice Cream (page 146)

MAKE THE PALM SUGAR CARAMEL AND PASSIONFRUIT ICE CREAM by following the recipes on pages 23 and 146.

Mix the coconut flesh with the flours.

In a separate bowl mash the bananas and durian together, then add the palm sugar, egg and coconut cream and mix well with a wooden spoon. Pour into a blender and process until the mixture is smooth.

Pour this mixture into the flour and coconut mixture, whisking until a smooth batter is achieved. Cover and let stand in the refrigerator for at least 1 hour.

Heat a non-stick pan until medium hot. Brush the surface with a little oil and spoon on some batter. Let the mixture bubble and brown as you would a normal pancake, then turn over and allow to lightly brown on the other side. Repeat with the remaining batter.

Place the pancakes on a serving plate and serve with the Palm Sugar Caramel and some Passionfruit Ice Cream.

palm sugar ice cream

MAKES 4 CUPS (1 LITER)

2 cups (500 ml) coconut cream
¾ cup (200 ml) milk
8 egg yolks

¾ cup (100 g) superfine (caster) sugar
⅓ cup (100 ml) Palm Sugar Caramel (page 23)

MAKE THE PALM SUGAR CARAMEL by following the recipe on page 23.
   Combine the coconut cream and milk in a heavy-based saucepan and bring to a boil.
   In a mixing bowl, beat the egg yolks and sugar until pale and thick. While stirring, pour the coconut cream mixture into the egg mixture and whisk together. Return the mixture to the saucepan over medium heat and stir with a wooden spoon until the mixture coats the back of a wooden spoon. Remove from the heat and allow to cool completely.
   Stir in the Palm Sugar Caramel and churn the mixture in an ice cream machine according to the manufacturer's instructions.

passionfruit ice cream

MAKES 4 CUPS (1 LITER)

2 cups (500 ml) coconut cream
¾ cup (200 ml) milk
8 egg yolks

1⅔ cups (200 g) superfine (caster) sugar
⅓ cup (100 ml) fresh passionfruit pulp

Combine the coconut cream and milk in a heavy-based saucepan and bring to a boil.
   In a mixing bowl, beat the egg yolks and sugar until pale and thick. While stirring, pour the coconut cream mixture into the egg mixture and whisk together. Return the mixture to the saucepan over medium heat and stir with a wooden spoon until the mixture coats the back of a wooden spoon. Remove from the heat and allow to cool completely.
   Stir in the passionfruit pulp and churn the mixture in an ice cream machine according to the manufacturer's instructions.

palm sugar caramel custard with grilled bananas

THE ADDITION OF FRESH TURMERIC IN THE CARAMEL GIVES IT A GOLDEN COLOR AND THE PANDANUS LEAF IMPARTS A FRESH, HERBAL TASTE. TWO TYPES OF PALM SUGAR ARE USED FOR THE CARAMEL IN THIS DISH: BLACK PALM SUGAR IS AN INDONESIAN ARENA PALM SUGAR; THE OTHER IS PALER AND HAS A LESS SMOKY FLAVOR. ALL ARE AVAILABLE FROM ASIAN FOODSTORES. YOU WILL NEED 6 CUSTARD OR CUPCAKE MOLDS FOR THIS DISH.

SERVES 6

6 ripe sugar bananas or 3 ripe normal bananas

Custard
6 duck eggs
2 cups (500 ml) coconut cream, plus extra for
    garnishing

1 teaspoon sea salt
1½ cups (375 ml) Palm Sugar Caramel (page
    23), plus 3 tablespoons extra for garnishing

MAKE THE PALM SUGAR CARAMEL by following the recipe on page 23.

Preheat the oven to 300°F (150°C). Place the 6 custard molds in a shallow cake pan.

TO MAKE THE CUSTARD, combine all the ingredients together in a mixing bowl. Mix well, then strain into a pitcher with a pouring spout. Pour the custard into the molds. To ensure a smooth top on the finished caramel skim off any bubbles that occur with a spoon. Add enough hot water to the cake pan to come halfway up the sides of the molds. Cover the top of the pan with a layer each of baking paper and foil to prevent steam or water getting into the custards. Bake for 35–40 minutes. Check after 35 minutes—the custards are ready when they have a firm jelly-like wobble and the tops are set.

Gently squeeze the bananas while still in their peel to soften the flesh. Set a grill to medium–high heat and grill until the peel blackens, about 3 minutes on each side. Take off the heat and discard the peel.

To serve, place a custard on a serving plate and the banana next to it. Drizzle with extra caramel and coconut cream.

tapioca pearls with mango and palm sugar caramel

SERVES 6

8 cups (2 liters) water
1 cup (150 g) dried tapioca pearls
1 cup (250 ml) Palm Sugar Caramel (page 23)
½ teaspoon sea salt

3 ripe mangoes, peeled, pitted and sliced
Coconut cream, to garnish
Fresh coconut, coarsely grated (optional)

MAKE THE PALM SUGAR CARAMEL by following the recipe on page 23.

Bring the water to a boil and add the dried tapioca pearls, stirring so that the pearls do not stick to the bottom. Simmer until the pearls become transparent with just a tiny dot of white left in the middle. Pour into a strainer and rinse with cold water to prevent the pearls sticking to each other.

Place the pearls in a mixing bowl and mix in enough caramel so that the pearls are just swimming. Add the salt.

Cut half a mango into slices and place in a serving bowl. Spoon over the tapioca and drizzle with some coconut cream and shredded fresh coconut. Serve.

tapioca pearls with coconut cream and palm sugar ice cream

SERVES 8

1 cup (150 g) dried tapioca pearls
8 cups (2 liters) water
1 cup (250 ml) Sugar Syrup (page 23)
½ cup (125 ml) coconut cream

1 tablespoon vanilla extract
1 tablespoon salt
Palm Sugar Ice Cream (page 146)

MAKE THE SUGAR SYRUP AND PALM SUGAR ICE CREAM by following the recipes on pages 23 and 146.

Bring the water to a boil and pour in the tapioca, stirring so that the pearls do not stick to the bottom. Simmer until the pearls become transparent with just a tiny dot of white left in the middle. Pour into a strainer and rinse with cold water to prevent the pearls sticking to each other.

Place the pearls in a mixing bowl and add the rest of the ingredients except the ice cream. Stir to mix through. Set the mixture in individual molds. Serve with the Palm Sugar Ice Cream

tropical trifle

THE LYCHEES WORK WELL WITH THE CREAMY COCONUT CUSTARD AND THE SMOOTH MANGO JELLY. FRESH
LYCHEES ARE SOMETIMES AVAILABLE FROM ASIAN FOODSTORES.

SERVES 8

One 18-oz (565-g) can lychees, drained, or
    20 fresh lychees, peeled and pitted
⅓ cup (100 ml) lychee liqueur
2 fresh mangoes, peeled, pitted and sliced

Mango Jelly
½ cup (60 g) superfine (caster) sugar
½ cup (125 ml) water
2 gelatin leaves
1 large mango, peeled and pitted, flesh
    puréed in a blender
1 tablespoon lychee liqueur

Coconut Custard
1¼ cups (300 ml) coconut cream

1¼ cups (300 ml) milk
8 egg yolks
¾ cup (100 g) superfine (caster) sugar

Pandanus Sponge Cake
2 pandanus leaves, finely sliced, or 2–3
    drops pandanus essence
3 eggs
⅔ cup (85 g) superfine (caster) sugar
1 tablespoon plain flour
⅔ cup (80 g) cornstarch
1 teaspoon cream of tartar
½ teaspoon bicarbonate of soda
⅓ cup (100 ml) lychee liqueur

Combine the drained lychees with the
liqueur and set aside for about 30 minutes.

TO MAKE THE MANGO JELLY, combine
the sugar and water in a heavy-based pan
and heat gently until the sugar melts.
Remove from the heat and add the gelatin.
Stir until the gelatin dissolves, then add the
mango purée and liqueur. Pour into a
shallow container and refrigerate for 1–2
hours until set.

TO MAKE THE COCONUT CUSTARD,
combine the coconut cream and milk in a
heavy-based saucepan and bring the mixture
almost to a boil.

In a separate bowl, whisk the egg yolks
and sugar together until thick and pale.
While stirring, pour the coconut cream
mixture into the egg yolks and whisk

together. Return the mixture to the saucepan over medium heat and stir with a wooden spoon until the mixture coats the back of a wooden spoon. Strain the mixture into a bowl and cool. Refrigerate for at least 1 hour.

TO MAKE THE PANDANUS SPONGE CAKE, first make a pandanus essence by blending the leaves with a little water in a blender or food processor. Strain the juice into a small bowl, discarding the solids. If using pandanus essence, omit this step.

Preheat the oven to 350°F (180°C). Grease and line a 10 x 12 in (25 x 30 cm) shallow cake pan.

Whisk the eggs and sugar until thick and pale. Sift together the flours, cream of tartar and baking soda, then gently fold into the egg mixture. Add the pandanus essence and stir through to get an even color. Pour into the prepared pan and bake for 18–20 minutes until the top is golden and the surface springs back when pressed.

Cool in the pan for 5 minutes before turning out onto a wire rack to cool. Drizzle the liqueur over the cake and set aside. When ready to assemble, cut the cake into cubes.

To assemble, first place some lychees in the base of a serving bowl. Next, add some cake and half of the Coconut Custard. Top with a layer of fresh mango and Mango Jelly. Repeat, leaving enough room at the top to garnish with fresh mango and lychees.

mango pudding with coconut

SERVES 8

4 ripe mangoes, peeled and flesh removed
8 tablespoons superfine (caster) sugar
4 tablespoons shaved palm sugar
⅓ cup (100 ml) coconut cream
1 teaspoon sea salt
1 teaspoon vanilla extract or ½ vanilla bean

Flesh of ½ coconut, grated into shreds (or use desiccated coconut, reconstituted with warm water and squeezed to remove excess moisture)
Coconut cream
4 tablespoons Palm Sugar Caramel (page 23)

MAKE THE PALM SUGAR CARAMEL by following the recipe on page 23.

Purée the mango flesh and place the purée in a heavy-based saucepan. Turn the heat to medium and stir continuously until the mango boils.

Add the sugars, coconut cream, salt and vanilla and continue to cook, stirring constantly until the mixture is thick and a dark yellow-brown color. The mixture is ready when the mango doesn't fall off the spoon when lifted from the mixture. This will take about 20 minutes after the sugars are added.

Oil a small baking tray and pour the pudding mixture into it and allow it to set. Remove the vanilla bean if using. When cool and set, cut the pudding into 1 in (2½ cm) squares and roll the squares in the fresh coconut shreds. Place on a serving plate and drizzle with coconut cream and the Palm Sugar Caramel.

Cocktails

Longrain Cocktails

At what moment does a craze start? Was it on the drawing board of the inventor of the yoyo, the hula-hoop or any of a million nifty inventions embraced by millions almost overnight? Is its mother really necessity? Or is it some divine confluence of timing, desire and market savvy?

When Longrain manager Justin Maloney picked up a hefty wooden rolling pin one day and thought, "Hmm, might make a good muddling stick", who could have known what he'd set in motion. At that moment the humble muddled cocktail made the quantum leap from just another way to mix a drink to wow—must have one of those!

Muddling is the essential technique in fashioning a Caipiroska, the lynchpin of Longrain's luscious cocktail list, the big city cousin of the Caipirinha ("peasant's drink" in Portuguese). The Caipiroska is a Longrain bestseller and is often credited as the cocktail at the heart of the "stick drink" revival.

The basic method for most of the cocktails is this: roughly chop a handful of fresh limes, put them in a short sturdy glass. Add raw sugar and a little sugar syrup. Get out the big stick and muddle those limes until their juices flow. Pour in a double shot of good vodka, add some ice, cover with a metal shaker and make like you're in the rhythm section of Tito Puente's big band. Upend back into the glass.

One of the simple philosophies of the Asian kitchen is balance. When you're using plenty of fish sauce and lime juice, you need to add a little palm sugar to even things up. And so it is with Longrain cocktails—fresh, seasonal ingredients and uncomplicated recipes.

We offer new takes on old classics, for instance the Rose Porteous, a cheekily rejigged version of the classic Suzie Wong. Or Longrain's emphatically Asian take on the Bloody Mary—vodka, lemon, Nahm Jim Sauce (a Thai sauce of chili and lime), coriander root and green chili with tomato juice, garnished with a sliver of cucumber.

And if bending the rules appeals, how about a flavored Martini? Ginger, apple, lychee or for the true bohemian, a Green Fairy, made with absinthe, bison grass vodka and lemon juice. Here's to love, truth and beauty, the Longrain way.

There are more than 50 cocktails on the Longrain list, including five "virgin" drinks, and not counting the nine vodka/gin variations offered on the standard Martini. Why have a standard "dry white" when you can tuck into a Ping Pong, Citrus Bitch or the new kid on the block, a My Thai, made with no fewer than three infused vodkas, lemon juice and mint?

Bartenders at Longrain are chosen for their dedication, attention to detail and creativity. Guys like Jules, Derrek, Martin, Rico, Sanchez and Jeremy have infused not just the house vodkas but the complete bar with their enthusiasm, deft touch and professionalism. Their influence at the beginning is still evident today in every drink made at the Longrain bar.

More than just marking time in a waiting room for the main event, enjoying a few drinks in the Longrain lounge-bar is an integral part of the dining experience. Peckish patrons can share a bar platter of nahm jim oysters, smoked trout on betel leaves, Thai fish cakes or grilled calamari while relaxing over a cocktail or three.

At Longrain, the living is easy.

Sam Christie

Bar Equipment

COCKTAIL SHAKER The Boston shaker is made of a stainless steel tin and a separate glass, and has a Hawthorne strainer. This is the preferred Longrain bartender's tool, but the more commonly available shaker with the built-in strainer and twist cap works just as well.

MEASURE/JIGGER Everything is measured in oz. A standard shot is 1 oz (30 ml), which is also the size of your standard shot glass.

GLASSWARE When making the Longrain cocktails in this book, you'll need three basic types of glassware:

• the classic stemmed martini glass
• the classic tumbler ("old-fashioned" short glass)
• the tall highball

Techniques

Muddling
When muddling drinks a variety of kitchen tools can be used, but generally a wooden pestle or the end of your everyday rolling pin can be used to "muddle", that is, to crush or bruise fruit, sugar, and herbs. Muddling helps to macerate and break down fruit pulp, and with fruit such as limes, muddling with their skins on helps to release the oils and flavors that are contained in the rind.

   Other equipment you'll need for muddling include a chopping board, sharp knife, ice cubes (the smaller the better), superfine (caster) sugar and Sugar Syrup (page 23).

Infusing
Spirits such as vodka, gin, tequila and vermouth can be flavored with spices, herbs, fresh fruit, chilies, chocolate, even gold leaf. Let the alcohol steep with the ingredients for a few days until the alcohol takes on the "essence" or flavor of the infusion ingredient.

   Begin with good quality spirit such as vodka. Start off with small batches so you don't waste the vodka while experimenting. Fresh ingredients are best, but canned fruit such as lychees can be used as the syrup can sweeten up the liquor.

   Pour ingredients into a clean 1 quart air-tight jar or container (reserve the vodka bottle for later use). Leave in a warm place (not directly in sunlight, but at room temperature), for 2–4 days. Shake the mixture several times during this period.

The great thing about infusions is that you can see and smell when it is ready and when it isn't. Taste until it reaches the desired strength. If the final result is too strong, dilute with neat, unflavored vodka.

Once ready, strain the liquid back into the original (or spare) vodka bottle. The infusion will produce a colored, flavored vodka ready for use.

Store the infused vodka in the fridge or freezer. Large bottles of vodka look great with the infusion ingredients in them. However, it is important that the ingredient be removed once the desired taste is achieved.

The following amounts are for when you are adding ingredients directly to a 1½ pint (700 ml) bottle of vodka.

- Blueberries: 15. Blueberry-infused vodka is used to make Purple Haze (page 161).
- Honeycomb: 5 teaspoons fresh honey or use fresh honeycomb that has been cut into small pieces. Honeycomb-infused vodka is used to make the Alinghi (page 160).
- Lychees: 8 fresh lychees. Used to make the Lychee Martini (page 160).
- Vanilla bean: 2, sliced down the center.
- Watermelon: 6 long slices.
- Raspberries or strawberries: 12 raspberries or 6 ripe strawberries, sliced.
- Cinnamon: 2 sticks.
- Cucumber: 1 whole medium cucumber, peeled and cut into long slices.
- Citrus: lime and lime rind.
- chili: 4 red bird's-eye chilies.
- Kaffir lime leaf and lemongrass: 3 kaffir lime leaves and 1 stalk lemongrass, tender inner part of bottom third only, bruised.
- Coffee: 20 roasted beans.

bloody longrain mix

MAKES 4 CUPS (1 LITER)

2 red bird's-eye chilies
4 coriander (cilantro) roots and stems
7 oz (200 ml) Red Chili Nahm Jim
     Sauce (page 14)
3¼ cups (800 ml) tomato juice (bottled
     or canned)

Combine all the ingredients in a
blender or food processor and pulse
well. Refrigerate and use the mix within
48 hours.

bloody longrain

MAKES 1

Ice
2 oz (60 ml) vodka
Bloody Longrain Mix (see recipe above)
1–2 cucumber spear
1 lemon wedge

Half-fill a high-ball with ice. Add the
vodka, then top the rest of the glass
with the Bloody Longrain Mix. Stir, and
garnish with the cucumber and lemon
wedge.

Bloody Longrain

Caipiroska

caipiroska

MAKES 1

1 large lime
1 teaspoon superfine (caster) sugar
Ice

2 oz (60 ml) vodka
$\frac{2}{3}$ oz (20 ml) Sugar Syrup (page 23)

MAKE THE SUGAR SYRUP by following the recipe on page 23.

Cut the lime into eighths (leave the skin on). Muddle the lime and sugar in a cocktail shaker. Add the ice, vodka and sugar syrup. Shake vigorously and pour into a tumbler.

To make a Caipirinha simply replace the 2 oz (60 ml) vodka with 2 oz (60 ml) Cachaca (Brazilian cane spirit). White rum or tequila can also be used.

ping pong

MAKES 1

4 fresh lychees, peeled and deseeded
Pulp of 1 ripe passionfruit
1 teaspoon superfine (caster) sugar
Ice

Juice of 1 lime wedge
$\frac{1}{2}$ oz (15 ml) Sugar Syrup (page 23)
$1\frac{3}{4}$ oz (50 ml) citron vodka
Dash of lychee liqueur (optional)

MAKE THE SUGAR SYRUP by following the recipe on page 23.

Muddle the lychees, passionfruit and sugar in a cocktail shaker. Add the ice, lime wedge, sugar syrup and spirits. Shake vigorously and pour into a tumbler.

camp bitch

MAKES 1

Half a large lime
Half an orange
1 teaspoon superfine (caster) sugar
$\frac{1}{2}$ oz (15 ml) Sugar Syrup (page 23)

Ice
$1\frac{3}{4}$ oz (50 ml) Campari
1 oz (30 ml) ruby red grapefruit juice

MAKE THE SUGAR SYRUP by following the recipe on page 23.

Cut the fruit into small chunks, leaving the skin on. Muddle the lime, orange, sugar and sugar syrup together in a cocktail shaker. Add the ice, Campari and grapefruit juice. Shake vigorously and pour into a tumbler.

alinghi

MAKES 1

1 kiwi-fruit, peeled
Half a fresh lime
1 teaspoon superfine (caster) sugar
Ice

1¾ oz (50 ml) honey-infused vodka
⅔ oz (20 ml) ginger liqueur or 6 thin slices
    fresh ginger

Muddle the kiwifruit, lime and sugar (and fresh ginger if liqueur is not available) together in a cocktail shaker. Add the ice and spirits. Shake vigorously and pour into a tumbler.

stickmata

MAKES 1

3 halved fresh strawberries
6 fresh raspberries
6 fresh blueberries
1 teaspoon superfine (caster) sugar

Ice
1¾ oz (50 ml) currant vodka (or infused
    berry vodka)
Juice of 1 lime wedge

Muddle the strawberries, raspberries, blueberries and sugar in a cocktail shaker. Add the ice, vodka and lime juice. Shake vigorously and pour into a tumbler.

lychee martini

MAKES 1

3 fresh lychees, peeled and deseeded
½ oz (15 ml) Sugar Syrup (page 23)
Ice

2 oz (60 ml) lychee-infused vodka
½ oz (15 ml) Pimms (optional)
1 peeled lychee (garnish)

MAKE THE SUGAR SYRUP by following the recipe on page 23.
   Muddle the lychees and sugar syrup in a cocktail shaker. Add the ice and spirits. Shake vigorously and strain into a chilled martini glass. Garnish with the lychee.

Purple Haze

Rose Porteous

purple haze

MAKES 1

1½ oz (45 ml) blueberry-infused vodka
½ oz (15 ml) vanilla liqueur
Juice of 1 lime wedge
1 oz (30 ml) apple juice
½ oz (15 ml) fresh lemon juice
Dash of Sugar Syrup (page 23)
Ice
5 fresh blueberries, to garnish

Combine all the ingredients in an ice-filled cocktail shaker. Shake vigorously and strain into a chilled martini glass. Garnish with the blueberries.

rose porteous

MAKES 1

4–5 small chunks watermelon
7–10 mint leaves
1 teaspoon superfine (caster) sugar
Ice
1¾ oz (50 ml) citron vodka
½ oz (15 ml) watermelon liqueur (optional)
Dash of fresh lime juice
Dash of cranberry juice
Dash of Sugar Syrup (page 23)

Muddle the watermelon and mint with the sugar in a cocktail shaker. Add a scoop of ice. Add the spirits, juices and sugar syrup. Shake vigorously and pour into a tumbler.

ginger martini

MAKES 1

4 small slices fresh ginger
½ oz (15 ml) Sugar Syrup (page 23)
Ice

2 oz (60 ml) vodka
½ oz (15 ml) ginger liqueur (optional)
Fresh ginger, very finely sliced (garnish)

MAKE THE SUGAR SYRUP by following the recipe on page 23.

Muddle the sliced ginger and sugar syrup in a cocktail shaker. Add the ice and spirits. Shake vigorously and strain into a chilled martini glass. Garnish with the strips of finely sliced ginger.

my thai

MAKES 1

4 thin slices ginger
8 mint leaves
½ oz (15 ml) Sugar Syrup (page 23)
Ice

1 oz (30 ml) cucumber-infused vodka
1 oz (30 ml) kaffir lime and lemongrass-
  infused vodka
⅔ oz (20 ml) chili-infused vodka
1 red finger-length chili (garnish)

MAKE THE SUGAR SYRUP by following the recipe on page 23.

Muddle the ginger, mint and sugar syrup in a cocktail shaker. Add the ice and spirits. Shake vigorously and strain into a chilled martini glass. Garnish by floating the chili in the drink. Do not eat the garnish!

Matching Wine with Thai Food

Our wine list has been carefully constructed to complement Martin's food. The list is white-dominated. We find that unwooded white varietals with good acid balance provide the best foil to spicy Thai food. We serve mainly Riesling, Gewürztraminer, Pinot Gris and Sauvignon Blanc, and lightly wooded spicy reds such as Pinot Noir, Grenache and Shiraz.

There are no set rules or traditions for matching wine with Thai food. Experiment and see what works for you. As a rule of thumb, it is best to drink unwooded or lightly wooded whites or reds with the food in this book.

We find white wines from cooler climates have good piercing acidity and therefore pair well with Martin's salads. White wines with a good acid structure and a little residual sugar or mid-palate sweetness adding to mouth feel are good matches for the food. Riesling, Gewürztraminer, Pinot Gris and Pinot Blanc from Alsace in France often fit the bill. Closer to home, Rieslings from the Eden and Clare Valley in South Australia or the Great Southern Region of Western Australia are consistently good with Asian food, and great value. Tasmania and New Zealand also produce stunning cool climate wines.

Changing hue, Rosés marry well with the strong flavors of the food. Pinot Noir, with its seductive funkiness and lovely fruit characters, can be a great match with poultry (especially duck) or lighter meats. Dishes such as the Caramelized Pork Hock with Chili Vinegar Dip (page 122) and the Crispy Chicken with Plum Sauce (page 136) are great matches for pinot noir.

Surprisingly, Sparkling Red is a good accompaniment to dark or more complex spiced curries such as the Mussaman or peanut curries.

Whatever your choice, it is important to drink the wine styles that you enjoy. If you like drinking big dry red wines, don't let the fact that you are eating a delicate salad stop you from drinking what you like. You probably won't even notice that they don't go that well together, especially if the conversation and company are good.

Finally, if wine doesn't do it for you, there is always beer. Beer is drunk everywhere in Thailand with every meal and beers such as Singha, Tiger, Tsing Tao, Asahi dry, Kirin and San Miguel are well suited to Asian food. Most of these brands are available at good liquor stores.

Sam Christie

Ingredients Glossary

ACIDULATED WATER Water that has lemon or lime juice added to it. Use to prevent fruit and vegetables turning brown once cut.

ARROWROOT FLOUR The arrowroot plant is grown for its fleshy round tubers, which produce an edible starch after processing. It is ground into a fine powder and is used in cooking as a thickener in much the same way as cornstarch is used. Unlike cornstarch, it will not develop a chalky taste if it is undercooked, however if it is overcooked, it will become thin and lose its thickening properties. When cooked, it is tasteless and becomes transparent, making it a good thickener for clear fruit sauces. It is often used to thicken glazes, fruit pie fillings, puddings, and sauces.

ASIAN WATERCRESS It is an aquatic herb with a vibrant, peppery flavor that is very much muted by cooking. Often added to soups, it does wilt to an insipid olive green, but imparts an interesting flavor.

BAMBOO SHOOTS Fresh shoots are available precooked and vacuum packed in refrigerated packets in Asian food stores. Canned shoots are less tasty but more common. Fresh uncooked shoots are sometimes available, and must  be boiled before using. The young shoots can differ in size greatly. If using fresh, boil the shoots whole in salted water for 2–3 hours, changing the water twice. When tender, remove and cool. Peel to the creamy center and cut into batons. Keeps for several days in salted water.

BANANA FLOWER The large purple flower of the banana tree, is used in salads and curries. Use a stainless steel knife as other metals discolor the flowers. Discard the outer purple petals until only the inner heart remains. Rub with lemon juice, then quarter the creamy heart lengthwise and remove the core. Finely slice the petals into long strands and keep in acidulated water for  2–3 hours. If you cannot find banana flowers, substitute fresh, crisp round cabbage leaves.

BANANA LEAVES May be deep green or very pale green, depending on the age of the leaves. Available in most Asian food stores, where they are sold by weight. They are used to wrap foods such as fish, meat and desserts or  for steaming, grilling and baking. The softer, more pliable leaves are best, but if you can only find older leaves, scald them in a tub with boiling water for 1 minute before use to soften.

BASIL, HOLY Purple-green leaves with a distinctive pungent, peppery taste, used in stir-fries, jungle curries and dry red curries.

BASIL, THAI A purple-stemmed plant with deep-green, purple-tinged leaves and small flowers. The leaves are used in salads and stir-fries for their fresh, sweet aniseed flavor.

BETEL LEAF Mainly used whole to wrap small morsels and snacks. They have a mild flavor with a little crunch. Torn betel leaves may be added to curries or pickled. If you cannot find them, use soft leafy lettuce.

BLACK BEANS Fermented black soybeans popularly used in Chinese cooking. They have a pungent, salty taste and are often used with garlic, and sometimes chili. Available canned in brine or dried and salted. In this book, I use the dried variety; wash before use to remove the excess salt.

BLACK CHINESE FUNGUS This is a Chinese ingredient used in some Thai dishes. It has no flavor but is used for its texture. It is a member of the mushroom family, available in dried form and looks like dried, black wrinkled paper. When soaked in water for about 10 minutes, it reconstitutes and resembles wavy seaweed or jelly. Stored in its dried form, it will keep indefinitely.

BLACK CHINESE VINEGAR Made from rice, wheat and millet or sorghum, the best black vinegars are well-aged and have a complex, smoky flavor similar to balsamic, which may be substituted. Chinese cooks add black vinegar sparingly to sauces, dips and when braising meats.

CARDAMOM Used sparingly in some Indian-derived curries. The most readily available are small green pods containing tiny, sticky black seeds with a pungent, camphor-like fragrance. Crush in a mortar and pestle to release their aromatic oils.

CASSIA OR CINNAMON BARK Related to cinnamon but with larger and thicker quills. It has a stronger flavor than cinnamon but cinnamon can also be used (most "cinnamon" sticks are actually cassia—real cinnamon is very small and very thin). Pound in a mortar and pestle before grinding in a spice grinder.

CHILIES, BIRD'S-EYE The smallest and hottest of the chilies used in Thai cooking, sometimes referred to as "scuds". Green chilies have a sharper, fresher flavor and ripen to become red. Dried chilies should not be used in place of fresh ones because the flavor is different.

CHILIES, FINGER-LENGTH About 2–4 inches (5–10 cm) long and may be green or red. Green chilies have a sharper, more peppery and herbaceous flavor than the red. In all chilies, the seeds and white membranes contain the most heat, and these may be removed according to taste and heat tolerance.

CHILIES, RED DRIED Used in all Red Curry Pastes. To use, snip off the sharp end with a pair of scissors, then run the blade up the side to open up the chili and scrape away the seeds. Dried chilies may be dry-roasted or rehydrated in warm water.

CHINESE BROCCOLI Also known as kailan or Chinese kale, it has long, narrow stems and leaves, and small edible flowers. The stems are the tastiest part while the leaves are slightly bitter and are often discarded. Chinese broccoli is available fresh in Asian markets. Substitute with broccoli stems or broccolini.

CHINESE CELERY A leafy plant that looks like coriander or flat-leaf parsley with a strong celery-like taste, and available in Asian grocers. Substitute finely sliced celery.

CHINESE KEYS (KRACHAI) I call it 'wild' ginger as there is no real translation for this rhizome. It sits in the same family as ginger and galangal. Chinese keys has an earthy, peppery flavor and is essential in jungle curries. It grows in finger-like clumps, and is sometimes available fresh from Asian grocers. It can also be purchased pickled in brine.

CLOVES Small, black, woody spices with a distinctive sweet-pungent flavor. Used sparingly in Indian-derived curries and soups.

COCONUT CREAM AND MILK Rich in texture and flavor, both are used extensively in Thai cooking. To make fresh coconut cream and milk, soak finely shredded coconut flesh in hot water, then squeeze through muslin or a tea-towel to extract the milk. Allow the liquid to settle so the cream rises to the top. A fresh coconut will yield around 1 cup (250 ml) coconut cream, regardless of the amount of soaking water used.

Also available in cans and tetra-packs, although the flavor is not as good.

COCONUT, FRESH Freshly grated coconut is obtained by grating fresh coconut flesh. Freshly grated coconut can be purchased in many Asian markets. Packets or cans of dried or desiccated coconut, both sweetened and unsweetened, are widely available in supermarkets. You can also grate them yourselves by following the instructions on page 73.

COCONUT, YOUNG These have a gelatinous flesh, with a texture similar to a melon, which can be scooped out with a spoon. They have a fresh, fruity almost nutty flavor that is not overly sweet. They are available fresh at fruit stalls in local markets throughout tropical Asia. A canned version is also available in supermarkets.

CORIANDER LEAVES Also known as cilantro, they are used extensively in Thai cooking for their unique spicy flavor. Select dark, green lush bunches with roots still attached. The roots are used to make Thai curry pastes.

CORIANDER SEEDS Small, light brown seeds of the coriander plant that have a clean, fragrant citrus flavor that is enhanced when roasted.

CUMIN SEEDS An essential component of many Asian spice blends, these tiny brown seeds have a strong, earthy, fennel-like flavor.

DRIED SHRIMP These add a unique, pungent, salty taste to stir-fries, salads and curry pastes. Select ones with an intense bright orange color.

DRIED SHRIMP PASTE A 'signature' flavor in Thai cooking, shrimp paste is added to all kinds of curry pastes, dressings and relishes. Fermented shrimp paste is a dense, brown, pungent paste that may be used raw or slightly toasted—either wrapped in foil and dry-roasted or toasted over a gas flame on the tip of a metal skewer or back of a spoon—to mellow its intensely fishy flavor.

DURIAN Also called the King of Fruits by aficionados in Southeast Asia, has attracted a cult-like following, but Westerners usually don't care much for its sweet oniony flavor. Once cut open, the durian gives off a strong odor. Look for it in Asian markets.

EGGPLANT, APPLE Round eggplant that may be green, yellow, orange or purple. Used in curries or salads.

EGGPLANT, LONG GREEN
These look similar to the long purple (Japanese) eggplant, which may be used instead if you cannot find the green one. Often served grilled or in stir-fries, curries, salads and relishes. Mild in flavor.

EGGPLANT, PEA Pea-sized dark green berries that grow in small clusters with a bitter flavor. Used in curries and relishes.

FENNEL SEEDS Small, greenish seeds with an intense liquorice flavor used in many Indian-style pickles, chutneys and breads.

FERMENTED BEANCURD
Made by fermenting pressed small cubes of beancurd with a red rice mold. Fermented beancurd may be flavored with chili, sesame oil or wine. May be eaten on its own or used (sparingly) in stir-fries, where it breaks down into the sauce to add a thick, creamy texture.

FISH SAUCE Considered the salt of Thailand, fish sauce is used in many savory dishes to add depth and character. It is made from small fermented fish such as anchovies. The clear brown liquid is bottled and most brands contain salt and fish juice. On its own fish sauce is rather pungent, and it is usually mixed with lime juice and palm sugar, where its saltiness is balanced by the sour and sweet flavors.

GALANGAL ROOT A rhizome from the same family as ginger and turmeric. It has a peppery,

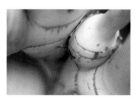

almost iodine-like aroma and is used in curry pastes and soups. Use young shoots if possible.

GARLIC CHIVES AND GARLIC FLOWERS Long, flat-leafed leaves sold in bunches with a distinctive garlic flavor. Also known as Chinese chives. The flowers may be eaten, too. Widely used in stir-fries or blanched and added to soups and salads. If you cannot find them, use green onions, or normal chives.

GARLIC, PICKLED Young garlic, pickled in a vinegary brine and sold in jars. It is used in curries and chopped into noodle dishes, salads and stir-fries.

GREEN ONIONS (SCALLIONS)
Also known as scallions, these long, green and white onions are used in salads, stir-fries and sauces.

GINGER ROOT A must in any kitchen, its sweet peppery taste lending itself well to Thai or other Asian dishes. Young roots are pinkish-white, with a translucent skin. These are preferred in Thai cooking as they have a milder flavor. Avoid ginger that is wrinkled and dry.

GROUND RED PEPPER Made from small red bird's-eye chilies. Dry-roast in a skillet or wok to slightly caramelize, then grind to a powder in a mortar and pestle or spice grinder.

HOISIN SAUCE A thick, sweet and fragrant sauce made from fermented soybeans, flavored with garlic, sesame and five-spice or star anise. It is mainly used in Chinese cooking with duck and pork.

KAFFIR LIME A round, knobbly, deep green citrus fruit, mainly used for its rind in curry pastes. The juice is very intense, and a little is sometimes added to fresh lime juice for use in dressings.

KAFFIR LIME LEAVES Dark glossy double-leaves with an aromatic citrus flavor, used to flavor curries and soups and may be finely shredded and mixed through salads. Fresh leaves are preferable, but frozen leaves will do in pastes and marinades.

LEMONGRASS A tall, lemon-scented stalk used extensively in Thai cooking. The tender, inner part of bottom third is finely sliced and used in curry pastes and salads. Scraps can be bruised and used to add flavor to soups and braises.

LONGAN A similar fruit to a lychee, longans grow in clusters. The fruit has a brown skin and sweet, crunchy, juicy flesh.

LOTUS ROOT A rhizome that looks like two or three sausages joined together! It is a starchy white root with a crisp texture that is retained when cooked. Lotus roots have a slightly sweet and nutty flavor. Peel and wash before use and cut into ½ in (10 mm) discs.

LYCHEE A summer fruit, and most varieties have a hard outer skin and a soft, moist, deliciously perfumed, white flesh and a large seed.

MACE BLADES The outer casing around the nutmeg with a similar taste but not as strong. Often used in curry pastes.

MORTAR AND PESTLE Essential for grinding fibrous roots, herbs and spices and to make wet and dry pastes and spice mixes. They come in all shapes and sizes, made from granite, stone and clay. If you have the time and patience to use one, the result will always be superior.

MUSTARD CABBAGE, PICKLED Mustard cabbage comes pickled in a salty brine and vacuum packed and is known as *kiam chye* in Southeast Asia or *xian cai* in China. Rinse well before use. At Longrain we then store them in a home-made brine, made by bringing equal amounts of sugar and white wine vinegar to a boil and infusing with chili, kaffir lime leaf and lemongrass. The mustard greens are added to the brine, returned to a boil and then transferred to an air-tight container. Pickled mustard greens make a delicious side dish and are also good added to stir-fried dishes. If you cannot find pickled mustard cabbage, use a bit of sweet sauerkraut instead.

MUSHROOMS, OYSTER These are fan-shaped mushrooms that are usually white or grayish-brown in color. They grow in clusters and are sometimes known as abalone mushrooms.

MUSHROOMS, SHIITAKE Also known as black Chinese mushrooms, they are large and meaty. Fresh shiitake are increasingly available in supermarkets although porcini mushrooms, or dried black Chinese mushrooms may be used as well. If using dried mushrooms, soak in hot water for 10 to 15 minutes to soften, then drain and discard the stems before dicing or slicing the caps.

OYSTER SAUCE This is often used in conjunction with fish sauce or soy sauce. Most brands of oyster sauce contain monosodium glutamate and therefore intensify the flavor of the dish to which they are added. Mushroom sauce or a combination of fish sauce and soy sauce is a good substitute.

PALM SUGAR A hard dense sugar made from the sap of the sugar palm tree, boiled down and set into discs. Palm sugar has a sweet almost treacle-like flavor. Many varieties are available from Asian grocers—Thai, Indonesian (gula  jawa), Malaysian (gula melaka). Unless specified, for the dishes in this book I use golden Thai palm sugar.

PANDANUS LEAF These dark green leaves come from the pandanus palm. They impart a wonderful fresh grassy flavor and a vibrant green color to desserts, and may also be used to perfume boiled rice and curries. Whole leaves are used to wrap food.

PAPAYA, GREEN The flesh of the green papaya can be shredded finely and soaked in iced water to give it a good crunch. Or cut into bite-sized pieces and added to soups and yellow curries.

PASSION FRUIT An oval-shaped, purplish-brown fruit that grows on a woddy vine, which climbs and clings to other forest plants in order to grow upward. The vine produces large white flowers and a fruit known as passion fruit. The fruit is ripe when it is soft and wrinkled on the outside and on the inside becomes golden colored with a watery and jelly-like textured flesh. Sweet yet somewhat tart in flavor, the flesh and seeds are edible but are generally used as a flavoring in beverages, ice cream, sorbets, jams, sauces, marinades, and fruit salads. Passion fruit nectar is a common beverage available in many food stores.

POMELO A large, yellow-skinned citrus fruit, similar to a grapefruit, pomelos have either yellow or pink flesh. Not as bitter as grapefruit and can be used in salads or desserts. Peel

as you would grapefruit; the large segments break away easily. Discard all the white pith and use only the flesh. If you cannot find it, use 2 large grapefruits but add more sugar to the dressing.

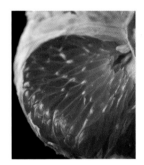

PRESERVED LIMES Popular in Thai cooking, and may be sweet or salty. Used whole in some soups and steamed dishes, and are available from Asian food stores.

RICE FLOUR Made from finely ground, long-grain rice, rice flour is mainly used to make desserts, wonton wrappers and noodles.

RICE NOODLE SHEETS Flat sheets made from rice flour, and soft in texture, are rolled into 'logs'. Dried shrimp or chives may sometimes be embedded in the rice sheets. It is a popular breakfast dish. The freshly steamed noodles are garnished simply with 2 or 3 different sauces, such as Hoisin (Chinese Plum Sauce), soy sauce and chili sauce and sprinkled with toasted sesame seeds.

RICE WINE Shaoxing wine is a strong-flavored Chinese rice wine used in stir-fries and braised dishes. Dry sherry or sake may be substituted.

ROCK SUGAR Large chunks of sugar that must be pounded in a mortar and pestle before use. It is a very pure sugar that dissolves to make a clear syrup. It adds a nice shine to sauces, braises and soups.

SALTED DUCK EGGS While techniques may vary from region to region, salted duck (and sometimes chicken) eggs are preserved by soaking the eggs in a salt brine (sometimes mixed with ground charcoal). The salt in the brine penetrates the shell by osmosis and hardens the egg yolk and imparts a salty flavor to the egg white. The preserved egg yolks are a common ingredient in Chinese moon cakes. Salted duck eggs may be purchased in mud-pack form or in brine in

Oriental markets. If in mud pack, scrape off mud, wash. The eggs should be boiled for about 10 minutes before being peeled. Compared to chicken eggs, these are larger, higher in fat, more colorful, and more flavorful.

SAWTOOTH HERB A long-leafed herb that grows in clusters with spiky-edged leaves. It tastes slightly stronger than coriander and is shredded into salads and hot and sour soups. It is commonly used in Vietnamese cooking.

SEA SALT This is available in fine or coarse crystals and is recommended for pickling and preserving. It is slightly milder in taste and preferred by many chefs over regular salt as it imparts a purer flavor to foods.

SESAME OIL Strongly flavored oil made from sesame seeds that is widely used in Chinese cookery, but should be used sparingly as too much can taste bitter. Best diluted with oil to make it less overpowering. It also burns very easily.

SHALLOTS Small reddish onions used in curries and braised dishes. They are often fried for use as a crisp garnish for salads, curries and grilled dishes. When making curries, you can substitute with purple or  Spanish onions. But for making Crispy-Fried Shallots (page 23), you need very small shallots that have very little moisture in them.

SICHUAN PEPPERCORNS The dried berry of the prickly ash tree, not related to ordinary peppercorns. They have a tingly, fiery, peppery flavor.

SOY SAUCE The brand of soy we use at Longrain—'Healthy Boy Formula 1'—is made from fermented yellow beans and is a lighter-style sauce. Soy sauce can be used as a substitute for fish sauce in recipes if you are a vegetarian.

SOY SAUCE, THICK SWEET Sweet Indonesian soy sauce also known as ketjap (or kecap) manis is a thick soy sauce made from fermented soybeans and brewed with palm sugar or molasses. I recommend the 'ABC' brand, which is from Indonesia.

TAMARIND Extracted from the pods of tamarind trees and compressed into dark-brown sticky blocks, tamarind is used as a souring agent in soups, salads, stir-fries and curries.

TAPIOCA, PEARLS Small transparent balls made from tapioca flour. Used as a thickener in some Thai dishes and as a dessert, where it is often flavored with sugar syrup and coconut cream. Do not rinse under water, or they will clump together to form a soggy mass.

TAPIOCA FLOUR Made from the cassava root, used in desserts, batters and as a thickening agent. If you cannot find it, use a mixture of rice flour with a bit of cornstarch added as a substitute.

TURMERIC ROOT A rhizome related to the ginger family, probably best known for its distinct yellow gold color and distinctive earthy flavor. Turmeric is available fresh and dried,  but are not interchangeable. Fresh turmeric is most commonly used as a vegetable. Dried turmeric is used in curry powders.

VINEGAR, BLACK Vinegar made from glutinous rice

and water, and aged for 10 years, used to give depth to braised dishes, stir-fries and soups. I recommend the brand 'Chen Kiang'.

VINEGAR, RICE A clear 'white' vinegar similar to regular white vinegar. Rice vinegar has a subtler taste and is not as strong as the Western white version. It is used in side dishes and stir-fries.

VINEGAR, SWEET Equal parts of white vinegar and sugar are mixed with coriander (cilantro) root and pickled garlic, brought to a boil and simmered until the sugar melts. Sweet vinegar is used in salad dressings and in side dishes.

WATER CHESTNUTS The corm of a type of underwater grass. Fresh water chestnuts are available at the end of winter and beginning of spring. They add a delicious crunch to stir-fries, and can be cut finely and used in fillings for spring rolls and dumplings.

WHITE PEPPERCORNS, Used as a dried spice ingredient in many curry pastes and braises. More commonly used than black pepper in Thai cookery.

WINGBEANS An unusual-looking bean with four distinctive ridges running along their sides. Wingbeans range in color from light to dark green. Top and tail as for normal beans. They may be eaten blanched or raw with relishes or added to salads, stir-fries or vegetable curries. If you cannot get them, substitute green beans.

WINTER MELON This is a member of the squash family. The white flesh has a mild flavor and is delicious in stir-fries and soup. Winter melon is available year-round in Chinese markets and specialty produce stores. Substitute with peeled and deseeded cucumber, or zucchini.

YARD BEANS Very long green beans, also called "long beans", cooked into curries or stir-fries or eaten raw in salads. Regular green beans (french beans) may be substituted.

YELLOW BEAN PASTE A paste-like sauce with the actual beans in it. I use this sauce in stir-fries or blend it to a smooth paste and add it to caramelized palm sugar to make dressings. I recommend the 'Healthy Boy Formula 1' brand.

Index

174

175

Acknowledgments

Grateful thanks to all of Longrain's loyal customers.

Thanks to Longrain's 'book' team: Sam, Jeremy, Mark, Foong Ling and Lindy Loo.

Thanks to the Longrain 'fathers'—John Sample and Leo Christie and Ros Sample, Justin, Jackie and Alicia. To all of Longrain's kitchen, restaurant and bar staff, and our long-term staff members—Lynley, Lewie, Fong, Zowie and Kitsana—thank you.

Thanks to my Mum and Ian, Oma and Opa.

Thanks to Longrain's long-term suppliers: Murdoch Produce, Demcos, Utopia Foods, Nicholas Foods, Pontip and Hong Lee. Thanks to Kasumi Knives.

Thanks to my fellow mentors and chefs: David Thompson, Alex Herbert, David King and Andrew Mirosch.

Sam would like to thank Nikki, his Mum Ann, Clive Smith and Jeremy Shipley.

Lindy would like to thank Vicki Wild for her guidance.

The authors and publishers are grateful to Hanimex's Jacques Guerinet and Deidre McAlinden for supplying us with Fujifilm Professional.

Thanks to Sam Robinson for her 'Longrain' range of handmade pottery, designed by Samsar Designs (samsardesigns@bigpond.com).

Thanks to Garrett Robinson for his fishy shot.

Thanks also to Sydney College of the Arts' Ceramic Department and Pioneer Studios.

Thanks to Rose Porteous.

Conversions & Equivalents

Metric units are used throughout this book. The approximate equivalents are as follows.

Dry Weights

10 g	⅓ oz
30 g	1 oz
50 g	2 oz
85 g/90 g	3 oz
100 g	4 oz
150 g	5 oz
185 g	6 oz
200 g	7 oz
250 g	8 oz
500 g	16 oz (1 lb)
1 kg	2 lb

Liquid Weights

1 metric teaspoon	5 ml
1 metric tablespoon	20 ml
1 US teaspoon	5 ml
1 US tablespoon	15 ml
¼ metric cup	62½ ml
½ metric cup	125 ml
1 metric cup	250 ml
4 metric cups	l liter (2 pints)

Note: The US cup is slightly smaller than a metric cup.

Oven Temperatures

100°C	210°F	Very slow	
125°C	240°F	Very slow	
150°C	300°F	Slow	Gas Mark 2
180°C	350°F	Moderate	Gas Mark 4
200°C	400°F	Moderately hot	Gas Mark 6
220°C	450°F	Hot	Gas Mark 7
250°C	475°F	Very hot	Gas Mark 9

Some equivalent terms

coriander	cilantro
cornflour	cornstarch
eggplant	aubergine
grill	broil
maryland	joined leg and thigh
minced beef	ground beef
plain flour	all-purpose flour
scallions	green onions